Autism and Loss

of related interest

Counselling People on the Autism Spectrum
A Practical Manual
Katherine Paxton and Irene A. Estay
ISBN 978 1 84310 552 7

Assessing and Developing Communication and Thinking Skills in People with Autism and Communication Difficulties
A Toolkit for Parents and Professionals
Kate Silver
With Autism Initiatives
ISBN 978 1 84310 352 3

Asperger Syndrome and Bullying
Strategies and Solutions
Nick Dubin
Foreword by Michael John Carley
ISBN 978 1 84310 846 7

Being Bullied
Strategies and Solutions for People with Asperger's Syndrome (DVD)
Nick Dubin
ISBN 978 1 84310 843 6

From Isolation to Intimacy
Making Friends without Words
Phoebe Caldwell
With Jane Horwood
ISBN 978 1 84310 500 8

The Complete Guide to Asperger's Syndrome
Tony Attwood
ISBN 978 1 84310 495 7

Relative Grief
Parents and children, sisters and brothers, husbands, wives and partners, grandparents and grandchildren talk about their experience of death and grieving
Clare Jenkins and Judy Merry
Foreword by Dorothy Rowe
ISBN 978 1 84310 257 1

Still Here with Me
Teenagers and Children on Losing a Parent
Edited by Suzanne Sjöqvist
Translated by Margaret Myers
ISBN 978 1 84310 501 5

Children Also Grieve
Talking about Death and Healing
Linda Goldman
ISBN 978 1 84310 808 5

Autism and Loss

*Rachel Forrester-Jones and
Sarah Broadhurst*

Jessica Kingsley Publishers
London and Philadelphia

First published in 2007
by Jessica Kingsley Publishers
116 Pentonville Road
London N1 9JB, UK
and
400 Market Street, Suite 400
Philadelphia, PA 19106, USA

www.jkp.com

Library of Congress Cataloging in Publication Data
Forrester-Jones, R. V. E.
   Autism and loss / Rachel Forrester-Jones and Sarah Broadhurst.
      p. ; cm.
   Includes bibliographical references.
   ISBN 978-1-84310-433-9 (alk. paper)
   1. Autism--Psychological aspects. 2. Loss (Psychology) 3. Grief. I. Broadhurst, Sarah, 1975- II. Title.
   [DNLM: 1. Autistic Disorder--psychology. 2. Adaptation, Psychological. 3. Caregivers. 4. Grief. WM 203.5 F731a 2007]
   RC553.A88F66 2007
   616.85'882--dc22

                                                                    2007013598

British Library Cataloguing in Publication Data
A CIP catalogue record for this book is available from the British Library

ISBN 978 1 84310 433 9

Printed and bound in Great Britain by
Printwise (Haverhill) Ltd, Suffolk

We would like to dedicate this book to the people we know with autism, and to all those who love and care for them.

Acknowledgements

This book is for people with autism and their carers/supporters. In writing this book we had two aims. First, we wanted to help carers and staff support people with autism to understand that experiences and feelings about loss are normal reactions. Second, we wanted to provide information and tasks which would help people with autism work through their losses at a level that makes sense. The book is not meant as a training manual since other agencies provide these. Rather, we hope that our book will be a support to those who are already helping others who experience loss.

We have enjoyed writing this book and have been very blessed with help from a wide range of people who have expertise in autism, psychology, palliative care and bereavement, mental health and special needs teaching. In particular we would like to thank David Oliver, Zoe Eastop, Rebecca Jones, Andrea Jones, Jacqueline Nicholson and Maria Hurman, for commenting on drafts of the book. A number of people on the autistic spectrum have contributed their stories and we would especially like to thank Katerina Marshall for sharing her invaluable insights into the world of autism and loss. The symbols we have used in the book were provided by Somerset Total Communication and we would especially like to thank them for their support.

We would also like to thank Paul Brush for his generosity and the Holywood Library, Northen Ireland for space and time while this book was being written.

Contents

List of Tables and Figures

Foreword

Loss affects us all in many ways – not only in bereavement of a loved family member or friend but in the everyday losses which occur, from losing an item of clothing to the loss of a role or function within our lives due to redundancy or illness. However, society often does not acknowledge these losses and people do not see them as important. There is a need both to acknowledge the losses and provide an opportunity to grieve, in the most appropriate individualized way for each particular person. For someone with learning disability or autism there may be even less acknowledgement of the loss and those surrounding them, and often those caring for them, may be unsure as to the significance of the loss and how best to help the person.

This book aims to help carers, whether family or professional, to help people with disabilities cope with loss. These losses may be diverse and complex – loss of relationships, of home, of role, of community, of wellbeing or in bereavement. The reactions of a person with learning disability or autism may be difficult to assess but the importance of accepting that the loss has occurred and helping the person cope with the loss is just as valid.

The worksheets aim to help professionals look at these issues in greater depth – for themselves and for those people for whom they are caring or helping. The reactions of someone may be varied and complex, especially as the way information and feelings are dealt with may be very different to what is seen as 'normal'. The reactions can also cause professionals to face their own losses and their own reactions, both in the present and from the past. These issues need to be faced and not ignored.

Grief and loss are often minimized by society and are often seen as a taboo, with others ignoring or avoiding the bereaved. Learning disability and autism often engenders the same reaction in society in general. There is a need to face up to these issues – as individuals, families, organizations and society. The authors, who have wide experience in the care and needs of people with learning disability and autism, will help us all to do just that.

Dr David Oliver
Consultant in Palliative Medicine at the Wisdom Hospice, Rochester, and Honorary
Senior Lecturer at the Kent Institute of Medicine and Health Sciences, University of Kent

Foreword

This book highlights a client group that has been overlooked in terms of recognition of loss. Although their losses may be diverse and individual this book reminds us that grief is not only associated with death, but that other forms of loss also require acknowledgement and support.

It is curious as to why so little has been written about loss and people on the autistic spectrum. In an attempt to redress this the authors have brought together a number of accessible resources that have been developed by themselves and others working within the field of learning disabilities and autistic spectrum conditions. The result is a collection of practical exercises and worksheets offering guidance to those supporting people on the autistic spectrum, suffering with loss.

Six types of loss are covered by the book including loss of material possessions; relationships; health; wellbeing; loss of role and finally death. Overall this book offers a number of good insights into this hitherto largely neglected area and a source to be consulted for worksheets appropriate across the range of abilities.

Zoë Eastop
Psychologist in Learning Disabilities, Kent and Medway National Health Service
and Social Care Partnership, and Honorary Lecturer in Learning Disabilities,
Tizard Centre, University of Kent

A note about terminology

The term 'autism' refers to the condition first described by Dr Leo Kanner (1943). The term 'autistic spectrum condition' (ASC) refers to a condition anywhere in the autism 'ball-park' including Asperger's syndrome (Asperger 1944). In this resource we use the terms 'autism' and 'ASC' to refer to autistic conditions in general. We use the term neuro-typical (NT) to refer to people without autism and we use the word 'condition' rather than the word 'disorder'. In both cases these are the preferred terms used by people with autism that we work with.

Chapter 1

Loss and Autism: Changing Ideas, Changing Reactions

Nothing that grieves us can be called little: by the eternal laws of proportion a child's loss of a doll and a king's loss of a crown are events of the same size.

Mark Twain, *Which was the Dream?* (1897)

Introduction

Last summer we attended a child's party held at our local beach. There were many children, lots of food and games, party hats and balloons. Towards the end of the party, the 'birthday girl' lost her balloon to the sea. She cried, seemingly inconsolable as she pointed to the balloon bobbing on the waves. Her mother gently rocked and cuddled her child, explaining that it was not possible to retrieve the balloon. After about half an hour the child stopped crying, became cheerful and played with her friends once again. She had successfully experienced a loss.

Within our lifetime we all experience loss. These losses may be huge and traumatic like the death of a loved one, or multiple, such as the loss of a home and possessions through fire. They may be relatively common, for example loss of school friends replaced by work colleagues, loss of hair and physical abilities during old age; or relatively small, such as the loss of a social acquaintance who has moved away. We might argue that whilst losses evoke strong feelings, so long as comfort and support is provided, losses can be successful and are necessary for us to grow and mature. Loss is a natural part of life (Long 2005), with death being the final non-negotiable loss, and whilst we may feel, endure and deal with loss in different ways, our reactions and 'coping strategies' are all part of the normal healing process (Long 2005).

In this resource we look at five major types of loss and how these can affect people with autism: loss of relationships, such as when a family relationship breaks down or a friend or a professional moves away (Chapter 2); material loss, for example the loss of a favourite belonging or home or loss of an enjoyed activity or familiar routine (Chapter 3); loss of role, such as worker, sibling, child or parent (Chapter 4); loss of health/functional loss, such as losing the ability to communicate or losing muscular or neurological functions of the body and loss of wellbeing, for example losing the ability to enjoy life or being able to cope with life (Chapter 5); and death (Chapter 6). Whilst we do not consider our list to be exhaustive, we feel that these five types of loss encompass a range of difficulties that people with autism in particular might face. Our book is an attempt to enable those caring for people with autism to understand and work through these losses.

In this introductory chapter we will discuss how theories of loss and grief within general populations have changed over time, provide definitions of autism, present a guide to the remainder of the book and some worksheets providing introductory exercises.

Who our book is for

As far as we are aware, this is the first autism-specific resource relating to loss to be published. We report and challenge generally accepted views in the field and highlight good practice. We have written the resource and materials in an accessible format for a cross-section of academic levels and it is designed to be used by both individuals and groups who are studying and/or working/caring in the area. In particular, we think that counsellors, educators/teachers, psychologists, healthcare workers and social workers will find it useful. Whilst the material in the main text is written in such a way that doesn't directly address people with autism spectrum conditions (ASC), it has been written in such a way that parents and carers will be able to access it.

At the end of each chapter we provide fact sheets summarizing each type of loss in relation to people with autism. Apart from being a kind of 'aide memoire' of the issues we discuss in detail in the previous text, these fact sheets may be photocopied and used as 'stand-alone' summaries for parents, educators and support staff without assistance as well as for some people with ASC with or without assistance. We also provide a range of worksheets with exercises and practical strategies to help carers/staff assist people with autism to accept and live with their loss. Again, these are appropriate for parents/carers to be used without assistance and the idea is for people with ASC to use them whilst being supported by others.

Changing ideas about loss

Prior to the 1960s there was little understanding of the emotional and psychological effects of loss. Loss was perceived in terms of relationships only (e.g. the death of a relative). Other forms of loss (e.g. separation, loss of limbs, loss of abilities) were regarded as unfortunate life events which people just had to cope with. Similarly, grief was regarded as a time of sadness caused by the death of a relative or friend, and mourning, a period of time during which the bereaved accepted the loss of their loved one and adjusted to life without them. Society's belief system in which 'loss' really only equated with 'death' endured from medieval times when death was unpredictable, uncontrollable but visible given the high mortality rate.

However, with each wave of scientific, biological and medical discoveries during the nineteenth century, pain and disease became more controllable (Lyttle 2001). Fewer women died in childbirth and life expectancy became longer. As death started to take place in hospitals rather than the family home, coping with loss became a private affair. The bereaved were taught not to 'speak ill of the dead' but also not to talk of experiences of grief. People were therefore socialized into avoiding expressing emotions connected with loss. Rather society constructed 'cultural myths' (Long 2005) to deal with emotions, including beliefs such as 'you've got to be strong', 'time will heal', 'cheer up', 'grieve alone'. People who were unable to 'cheer up' would be classified as having a depressive illness. There was therefore a tendency to institutionalize death and over-medicalize/profession-alize core human experiences of grief and grieving.

Theories from psychiatry

The psychiatrist Kübler-Ross (1970) developed a more systematic study of grief in an attempt to acknowledge emotions connected with bereavement and to help people resolve loss in a healthy manner. Kübler-Ross described five stages of grieving: denial, anger, bargaining, depression and acceptance. She argued that people do not move through these stages logically, and that it can take up to two years for people to work through their grief.

Psychoanalytic theories

This typology of grief tied in with 'attachment theory' developed by Bowlby (1944, 1951). Following the psychoanalytic approach of Freud in 1917 (Freud 1961) and through his studies of juvenile delinquents and young children, Bowlby explained how as infants, we are naturally pre-programmed to need continuous emotional and physical at-tachment to our mothers. We show this need using attachment behaviour (e.g. crying, clinging, reaching out, aggression when separated or smiling when re-united). Robertson (1953) and later Parkes (1970) argued that when this biological bond is broken, set reactions within three stages occur. In the first stage aggressive and/or tearful behaviour occurs reflecting an attempt to re-establish the child–mother relationship. The second stage is characterized by sadness and a 'mourning-type' behaviour including sobbing. This marks the beginnings of an acceptance of the loss. The final stage is one of adjustment to the world without the loved one. This does not necessarily mean that the person has 'got over' their loss; rather that ways of coping with the loss have been found. Attachment patterns were thought to develop differently in response to social environments. For example, Bowlby (1944) found that the most psychologically disturbed juvenile delin-quents had experienced separation from their mothers at an early age and as a result had been deprived of maternal love. Bowlby (1951) and Marrone (1998) also argued that inse-curity of attachment would be increased when threats of abandonment or punishment occurred.

Psycho-social theories

Later, writers including Parkes (1993, cited in Currer 2001) argued that some losses bring about profound changes (called psycho-social transitions) to the social environment of the individual which (a) are lasting, (b) take place over a short period of time leaving little opportunity for preparation and (c) require major revisions of previous assumptions of the world. Worden (1991, pp.10–17) referring specifically to death took on a more task-orientated view of grief, stating that people need to 'work through' their loss by completing the tasks of mourning including: accepting the reality of loss; working through the pain of grief; adjusting to an environment in which the deceased is missing; and finding a safe place for the deceased in emotions and moving on with life.

Sociological theories

Most recent theoretical understandings of grief have been more sociological (Walter 1996) and grounded in the views of service users (e.g. Klass, Silverman and Nickman 1996). These new theories critique previous views of loss for ignoring the importance of cultural and gender variation in grieving which Stroebe and Schut (1998, 1999) argue can easily become the basis for practice that is unconsciously genderist and racist. For example, black social workers (Gambe *et al.* cited in Currer 2001) argue that Bowlby's attachment theory incorporates a eurocentric (and gendered) view of child rearing. Stroebe, Stroebe and Hansson (1993) further suggest that since 'grief work' is not a universal concept, it may not be appropriate in every instance of grief. For example, Wortman and Silver (1989) argue that rather than working on the task of 'finding a safe place for the deceased in emotions and moving on with life' with failure to do so seen as a sign of pathological grief (reflecting the medical nature of grief theory), some cultures actively encourage continuing involvement with the deceased person. A tendency to pathologize aspects of grief may therefore be viewed in sociological terms as a way in which 'grief experts' regulate the grieving process in Western society (Walter 1999).

Walter (1994, 1999) further adds to these theories by suggesting that the purpose of grief is not detachment from the loss but rather 'finding an appropriate place' for the loss in the lives of survivors. Therefore where possible, talking with others who knew the dead person or experienced the same 'story' of life, in for example a care home, is crucial in getting over the loss/change. Within loss through death, the funeral is a significant forum in which to talk about the lost person with others (Walter 1996), and letters of condolence or simple expressions of sorrow help in the process of 'relocating' the loss. When participation in rituals, such as attending a funeral or talking about life as it was in a previous setting, is limited or barred, then grief can be blocked.

Psychological theories

Traditional beliefs about supporting somebody experiencing grief have tended to focus on the individual, leading to an emphasis on one-to-one counselling, neglecting the social context and emphasizing 'detachment' and 'moving on' from the loss as the major goal.

However, Stroebe and Schut (1998, 1999) offer a more comprehensive 'dual process' model for understanding bereavement and how to support it, which involves two psychological (emotional) challenges of (a) coping with the loss experience itself and (b) coping with other more practical changes that result from it. The two processes, which involve both positive and negative thoughts, are namely 'loss orientation' when the grieving person will focus on what has gone (including negative feelings of yearning and positive memories as time passes); and 'restoration orientation' with its focus on present tasks and new challenges for the future.

Fundamental to this model is the notion of swinging between coping with these two processes and avoiding them. Whilst both aspects are necessary for adjustment and restoration, complicated or pathological grief involves a focus on one or the other process. For example, a person may not seem to focus at all on the loss of their parental home and appear to carry on as normal, whereas another person might focus on the loss of their previous home to the exclusion of important practical tasks and changes needed for readjustment to their new environment.

This model of grieving takes into account gender (suggesting that women are more oriented to loss and men to restoration, which might explain relationship problems) and also culture (with certain cultures specifying that one or other orientation is more acceptable or appropriate) (Currer 2001). For example, in the case of loss through death in a Hindu family, failure to attend the funeral of someone who was simply a social acquaintance is a serious social transgression; whereas a middle-class Anglican funeral is often seen as a private family affair (Parkes, Launganik and Young 1997). Similarly, in a comparative study of two Muslim countries, Wikan (1988) found a complete absence of any emotion in one society but prolonged crying in another. Finally, in Stroebe and Schut's model, avoidance or taking 'time off' from mourning is a legitimate part of grief. This dual model therefore offers a useful structure in which to understand grief in an empowering, non-oppressive, non-ethnocentric or non-eurocentric way. Currer (2001) argues that it is particularly useful for social care workers who spend much of their time helping people with practical matters rather than emotional issues. Problems arise when for example the challenge of restoration orientation is thwarted by discrimination (e.g. when a person is trying to adjust to moving from their parents' home to a residential home only to face discrimination in their new environment).

In summary, people, including those with autism who have experienced loss, will face a mixture of emotions (including anger and sadness) and challenges of both feelings about the loss and changes that occur as a result of the loss. If they are not provided with adequate information and support (including sympathy and empathy), or if they are restricted or disallowed from participating in requisite rituals or given space and 'time out' from grief, they will be unable to mourn properly or successfully deal with their loss. This may especially occur if carers/professionals do not appreciate cultural and gender variation. If loss is unresolved, then grief can become complicated (Marrone 1998), leading to clinical depression and a need for professional help such as counselling (Blackman 2003; Bloom 2005). Finally, our search of the literature in relation to loss in general only found reference to grief associated with death. Other types of loss were either not mentioned or the source of very brief comment. Further, we found almost no reference to loss of any kind in relation to people with autism (apart from two chapters in John Clements' book *People with Autism Behaving Badly* (2005) which deals with loss of social connectedness and loss of social wellbeing). We believe this absence of discussion about loss reflects a general lack of recognition by society and professionals of these losses as life events for which people might need care and support. We hope that this book will help carers of people with autism to understand these losses and to provide support for those experiencing them.

What is autism?

There is still debate and confusion among clinicians and researchers over the causes, diagnosis and categories of autism (Vermeulen 2000), since these seem to vary between individuals. However, it is generally agreed that autism is a condition which is the consequence of a hereditary disorder of the brain or problems at birth or brain damage or disease (Frith 1989, 1991) in that the brain works but functions differently from how it would without autism. People with autism and those without will generally receive and process information in different ways. Therefore people with autism may think differently and because of this they may sometimes experience limitations and difficulties in common activities. Whilst people with autism do not look any different from other people, they may relate, communicate, act and react in a different way.

Whilst research continues to try to understand the causes of autism, diagnosis of the condition is based on behaviour. International experts have agreed on the range of behaviours which constitute a diagnosis of autism, including the International Classification of Diseases (ICD-10) (World Health Organization 1987). Instruments to help diagnose autism include the Diagnostic Interview for Social and Communication Disorders (DISCO) (Wing *et al.* 2002), which records the agreed range of behaviours commonly known as the 'triad of impairments' (Wing and Gould 1979). We present these behaviour impairments below (Table 1.1), giving general examples of each according to researchers (e.g. Attwood 1998; Clements 2005; Lawson 2001), people who have written about their ASC (e.g. Mitchell 2005; Tammet 2006) as well as people with ASC who have talked to us. However, please note that it is difficult to generalize about behaviours of people with autism since each individual is along an autistic spectrum (each has different abilities) and is unique with their own interests, personality, capabilities, talents and level of intelligence. Therefore not everyone will have the same types of impairments as we describe them below.

Table 1.1 Triad of impairments

Impaired behaviour	Examples of impairments/abilities
1. Social behaviour (including social interaction and socialization)	*Impaired ability to:* • greet others • start conversations • keep eye contact • smile • talk about feelings/emotions • have empathy for others • be aware of various social rules or adjust behaviours in response to social rules
2. Communication	*Difficulties with:* • literal interpretations of language (e.g. a greeting of 'Can I take your coat?' at a social occasion might be interpreted by someone with ASC as 'They want to keep my coat for ever') • asking for help/expressing problems • appreciation of social uses and pleasures of communication • talking (too loudly or too quietly)
3. Flexibility of thought	*Tendencies of:* • attention to detail, difficulty seeing the bigger picture • adoption of rigid routines (e.g. when dressing, always has to put socks on first before trousers) • ritualistic behaviour • difficulty accepting and coping with change • obsessive interests (e.g. food, trains, etc.) • difficulties with imagination (prone to let imagination run wild) and/or internalizing own thoughts • exhibiting sensitivity to and shock at criticism or negative remarks

The patterns of behaviour listed in Table 1.1 are useful for diagnosing autism. However, they don't tell us *why* people with autism behave in the way that they do. To understand autism properly we need to think about some of the underlying difficulties people with autism have which may explain some of the behaviours shown in the table. We describe these difficulties below. Again, please note that for every individual, difficulties experienced in each of these areas can be the result of very different underlying causes (Williams 2006).

Difficulties with mono-attentive and delayed information-processing

Most neuro-typical people (NTs) tend to be multi-tracked/multi-attentive. This means that they can receive and process a variety of information from a number of senses at the same time. For example they can watch TV, listen to what is being said and keep track of the meaning; during conversations they can usually speak, think, pay attention to what their own body is doing and how it is moving including facial expression, whilst at the same time listening to and monitoring the other person's body language.

However, most people with an ASC tend to be (to a lesser or greater extent) mono-tracked. If you are mono-tracked you will struggle to listen and look at the same time. When focusing on what is being said, it may be almost impossible for you simultaneously to interpret the body language or facial expressions of the other person. It will be difficult to monitor what your own body is doing, how it is moving and respond to its needs (e.g. use the toilet or drink something) whilst trying to concentrate on the other person's actions.

If you can only process one bit of information at a time it means that the speed at which you process information is very slow. Furthermore being mono-tracked means that you constantly miss information and never get the full picture. As a result the world seems confusing and unpredictable and you often misinterpret the situations and people around you. This often leads to feelings of anxiety, paranoia, frustration and anger. Clearly if you are mono-attentive you will have problems with communicating, socializing and with flexibility of thought as detailed in the Triad of impairments (see Table 1.1).

Sensory difficulties

People with autism are often super sensitive to specific stimuli in their environment. For example they may be able to hear things that others cannot hear or which cannot be seen and smell things that others cannot smell. These sensitivities can sometimes be pleasurable, but often they are distracting, distressing and even painful. Examples include the hum of computers, fridges, air-conditioning; the flicking of fluorescent lights; the smell of cleaning fluids; and the taste, texture, sight or smell of certain foods.

Whilst hypersensitivity to stimulation is not something new in the field of autism, it has tended not to be the focus of scientific research. Similarly, the implications of being hypersensitive to stimuli on behaviour have rarely been recognized or dealt with. This is despite the fact that the extreme distress and pain caused by such sensitivities can lead to anxiety, stress and loss of behavioural control, with people often retreating into their own worlds as a way of coping. Difficulties with sensory issues also have a detrimental effect on development. Again it is easy to see how sensory issues can result in the behaviours detailed in Table 1.1.

Difficulties with anxiety leading to obsessive/compulsive/ritualistic behaviours

Many people with an ASC engage in obsessive/compulsive and/or ritualistic behaviours to a greater or lesser degree throughout their life span (see Table 1.1, no. 3 Flexibility of thought). It is generally recognized that there is a link between levels of anxiety and engagement in such behaviours (i.e. high anxiety will result in an increase in obsessive behaviour). The word 'obsession' is often used in association with the label 'autism' and seems to be used to refer to any type of repetitive behaviour. However, obsessive behaviour is different from compulsive behaviour, which is different again from ritualistic behaviour. It is important to distinguish between these behaviours when working with individuals as the type of behaviour and underlying reasons for it should determine our response. Clements and Zarkowska (2000) define the three types of behaviour as follows.

- **Obsessions**: Hobbies and/or special interests in particular activities or things (e.g. horse riding; clocks; fishing; counting things). Such activities can relieve stress that originates elsewhere (i.e. it is an engagement that relaxes someone when they are anxious or stressed).

- **Compulsions**: Behaviours that are engaged in to relieve distress. There is a sense that only this behaviour will do, no other form of stress relief will be good enough. The relief will only be short term so the behaviour will soon be repeated (e.g. washing of hands, scratching, cutting skin or paper or something else).

- **Rituals**: Behaviours that are engaged in so as to relieve the strain of information-processing. A ritual is a predictable routine that one can engage in without having to think. It is comfortable when things are 'just so' and uncomfortable when they are not. Examples might include always putting on particular items of clothes in the same order.

Naturally engagement in these behaviours can result in a range of difficulties for those supporting people with autism. It must not be forgotten, however, that these behaviours are coping techniques (some pleasurable, some distressing) used to relieve some underlying anxiety, and it is important that carers attempt to identify the underlying reasons why people with an ASC are engaging in the behaviour rather than simply trying to prevent it.

In the following diagram (Figure 1.1) we show how causes and resultant difficulties lead to impaired behaviours. Whilst we cannot see the causes or difficulties (represented by the white and light grey circles), we need to know about them since they lead to behaviours which we can see (presented here in the dark grey circle). Some behaviours (e.g. obsessive) will increase the difficulties (e.g. stress) people with autism have. We therefore need to look at the whole picture in order to understand autism.

People with autism do not always understand these differences and difficulties and are often misunderstood by the communities in which they live. Society also disables people with autism by either excluding them completely or failing to provide the necessary support needed for participating in everyday physical and social activities. The following case study illustrates this point.

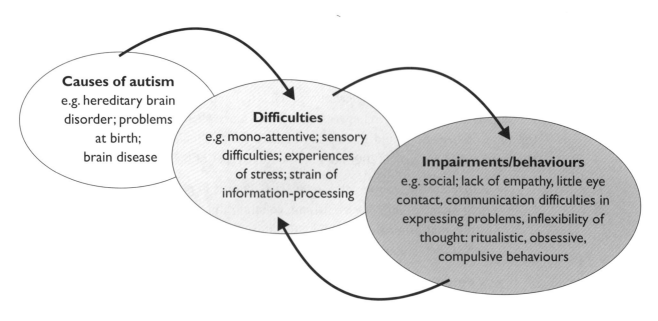

Figure 1.1 Causes, difficulties and outcome behaviours in autism/ASC

Case study – John

John, a 15-year-old boy, is very interested in clocks and time. This coincides with his need to know in advance what's going to happen, where, when and with whom. He is also very punctual; starting and stopping in time are very important to him and he will finish his breakfast and be ready for school at the same time every morning. He collects clocks and watches of all kinds and stores them in his bedroom in a particular order on a shelf. He rarely loses any of his collection, but on one occasion his younger brother mixed up the order of the clocks. John found this very distressing and started screaming and banging his arm against the wall until his parents could somehow calm him down. He talks about clocks most of the time and it is difficult to get him to talk about anything else. This proves problematic at school since although John is clearly intelligent, he often finds it difficult to move on from the subject of clocks to another subject (e.g. maths, sport or music). John also tends to relate only to his peers and other adults using his pet subject. If he meets someone for the first time he will immediately point and want to touch their watch or the clock in their house. He seemingly has no other interest, and this makes for difficult listening to anyone he meets and interacts with for more than about five minutes. Consequently some of his school colleagues think him rather boring and others think he is stupid. He has few friends and tends to be excluded from play-ground team games. He has been called names by his peers. When this occurs, John has tended to become upset and angry, venting his frustration on his parents and especially his younger brother. Although he has a learning support assistant for each class in his school, the head teacher has suggested to John's parents that he be excluded and sent to a 'more specialist school'.

Changing views about autism and loss

Long (2005) argues that society has been slow to recognize and appreciate that people with autism experience the pain of loss in similar ways to other people. Read (2006) goes so far as to say that we have inherited a legacy of thinking that people with learning disabilities in general are incapable of feeling loss. We therefore tend to view their grief as invisible (Conboy-Hill 1992) or as an illness or think that they are disturbed when actually they are simply facing the same issues that we all face. Professionals have been reported to find breaking news about loss and supporting people to deal with it a difficult task (Barnett 2002; Bloom 2005; Buckman 1992; Todd 2005) to the extent that they will often shy away from doing it. Consequently, there has been little in the way of providing help to support loss experienced by people with autism.

However, research has shown that people with autism have the ability to express emotional behaviour due to loss, through a mixture of sadness, anger, anxiety, confusion and pain (Harper and Wadsworth 1993).

In Figure 1.2 we have created a diagram using an amalgamation of old and new theories concerning the stages of grief (including Cathcart 1994a, 1994b, 1994c; Hollins and Sireling 1999; Kübler-Ross 1970; Long 2005; Parkes 1993; Stroebe and Schut 1999; Tuffrey-Wijne, Hollins and Curfs 2005; Worden 1991) and indicated how these might be experienced by people with autism. As stated above, not everyone will go through each stage in sequence and all stages are interrelated. Furthermore it needs to be remembered that additional factors which will affect a person's reaction to loss include age, personality, gender, previous history, closeness of relationship, type of loss and how the 'goodbye' was expressed.

The aim of the remainder of this resource is to look at how the experiences including thoughts, feelings and behaviours associated with each stage of loss impact on people with autism. The objective of the fact sheets and worksheets is to enable people with autism to be supported to work successfully through those experiences. To this end we present a guide to using them.

Guide to using the fact sheets and worksheets

As stated earlier, the fact sheets are primarily intended for family/carers/staff/supporters of people with autism, but are also written in such a way as to be accessible for some people with autism. Similar to the worksheets with exercises provided in this resource, the fact sheets may require certain language skills and abilities on the part of the person with autism. However, there is no maximum chronological age limit and the fact sheets and worksheets can be adjusted for people with a range of verbal and cognitive skills.

Therefore we do not prescribe that you rigidly stick to the exercises provided. Rather, we include activities we have developed, tried and tested in our workplaces. The ones we present here were all found to work well for different individuals with autism and we suggest that you adapt them (including content and format) to suit the needs of the person you are caring for, bearing in mind that what is right for one person might not be for another and what is written on paper transfers differently to real life.

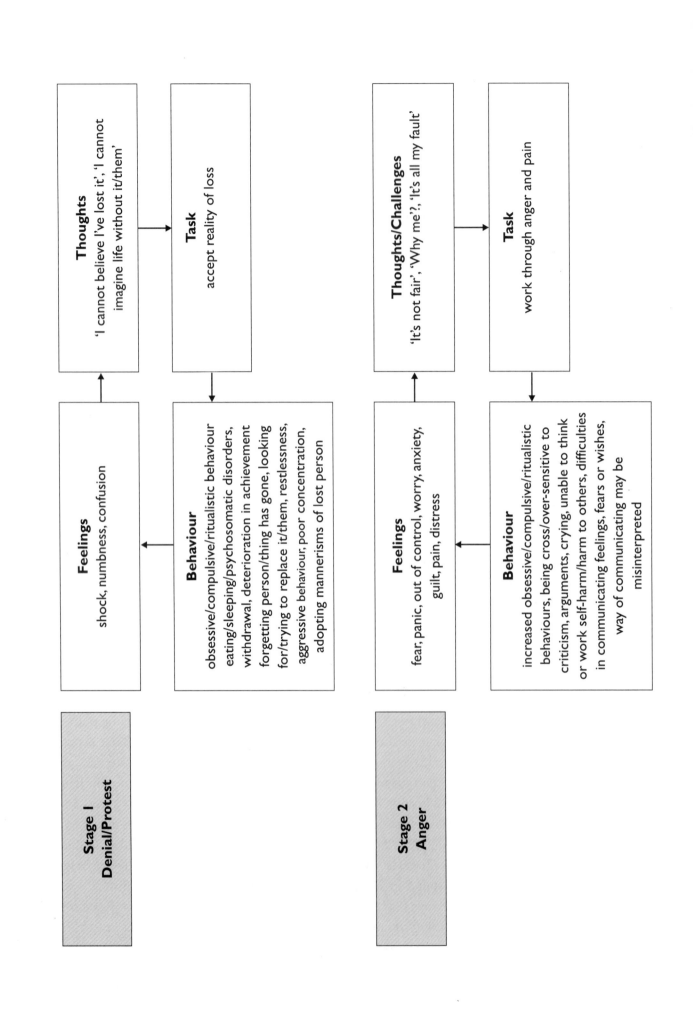

**Stage 1
Denial/Protest**

Feelings
shock, numbness, confusion

Thoughts
'I cannot believe I've lost it', 'I cannot imagine life without it/them'

Task
accept reality of loss

Behaviour
obsessive/compulsive/ritualistic behaviour eating/sleeping/psychosomatic disorders, withdrawal, deterioration in achievement forgetting person/thing has gone, looking for/trying to replace it/them, restlessness, aggressive behaviour, poor concentration, adopting mannerisms of lost person

**Stage 2
Anger**

Feelings
fear, panic, out of control, worry, anxiety, guilt, pain, distress

Thoughts/Challenges
'It's not fair', 'Why me'?, 'It's all my fault'

Task
work through anger and pain

Behaviour
increased obsessive/compulsive/ritualistic behaviours, being cross/over-sensitive to criticism, arguments, crying, unable to think or work self-harm/harm to others, difficulties in communicating feelings, fears or wishes, way of communicating may be misinterpreted

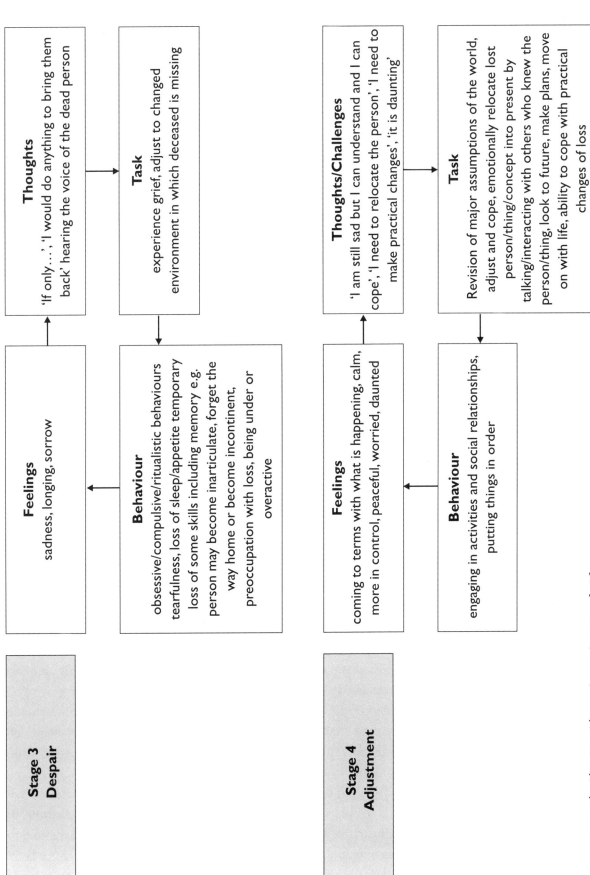

Stage 3
Despair

Thoughts
'If only...', 'I would do anything to bring them back' hearing the voice of the dead person

Feelings
sadness, longing, sorrow

Task
experience grief, adjust to changed environment in which deceased is missing

Behaviour
obsessive/compulsive/ritualistic behaviours tearfulness, loss of sleep/appetite temporary loss of some skills including memory e.g. person may become inarticulate, forget the way home or become incontinent, preoccupation with loss, being under or overactive

Stage 4
Adjustment

Thoughts/Challenges
'I am still sad but I can understand and I can cope', 'I need to relocate the person', 'I need to make practical changes', 'it is daunting'

Feelings
coming to terms with what is happening, calm, more in control, peaceful, worried, daunted

Task
Revision of major assumptions of the world, adjust and cope, emotionally relocate lost person/thing/concept into present by talking/interacting with others who knew the person/thing, look to future, make plans, move on with life, ability to cope with practical changes of loss

Behaviour
engaging in activities and social relationships, putting things in order

Figure 1.2 How people with autism might experience various stages of grief

Furthermore, as with any task or activity, the carer's approach and style of communicating with an individual with autism is of greater importance than the exercises themselves.

We also acknowledge that supporting someone through any loss is no easy task. It takes time and effort, and the work/activity you do with a person with autism may not produce immediate or expected returns. Empathizing with people who are in situations they are powerless to change, and who have deep disappointments, is difficult.

However, we believe that people who wish to support someone with autism do not necessarily need to be formally trained to be able to listen in a caring and supportive way to a person in distress, or to find appropriate ways to help them through what are essentially ordinary life experiences. Therefore this book is not about treatment or therapeutic methods. Rather, it is meant simply as a tool for giving information, ideas and examples of methods we think may be of some help.

A note about illustrations and communication

Since the ability to communicate using a commonly understood language is fundamental to the way all human beings function in society, it follows that those who are unable to do so are automatically excluded…communication is a fundamental right, the denial of which to any individual constitutes an undervaluing of him or her.

(Jones 2000, pp.20–21)

Social inclusion without shared communication is impossible (Jones 2000). Yet many people with autism also have communication difficulties or have their own non-verbal way of communicating. This calls for the use of more flexible communication strategies including non-speech modes to supplement or substitute for verbal communication.

For over a decade, Somerset Total Communication (STC) (originally an Industrial and Provident Society and since 2002 a joint strategy between Somerset Partnership NHS and Social Care Trust, Somerset County Council and partner agencies) has been generating resources, information and training for service users and staff in order to meet the communication needs of people with learning disabilities, including people with autism. Speech and language therapists have co-operated and collaborated across agencies, professions and services to provide local and individual person-specific language. The basic approach is one which allows several ways of representing the same word including signs, symbols, photographs, videos, objects of reference and IT software with national sources (including British Sign Language and National Rebus Collection) used wherever available and suitable. For further details please consult their website: www.somerset.gov.uk/somersettotalcommunication.

STC have very kindly given us permission to use their images in this resource. We have chosen to use symbols to represent words in our fact sheets and exercises. Please note, we use these symbols for illustrative purposes only. The symbols provided may be helpful for some individuals – but communication modes need to be adapted to individual needs. We have therefore left space at the side of each fact sheet and exercise so that the professional or informal carer working with a person with autism can generate appropriate individualized signs, symbols, photographs or pictures (or whatever works best for the person with autism) and insert them.

Copyright rules

This book is designed to be used, and so you can copy the fact sheets and worksheets with exercises so long as they are for use by yourselves working with people with autism. Any other copying or duplicating of the text and worksheets is subject to the usual copyright rules.

Informed consent and ethical considerations

We have noted that many training packs, guides and books of activities do not address ethical issues, especially those relating to consent. Attention to such issues should not be regarded as a given and recent legislation highlights this. For example, in the US, the Office for Human Research Protections (OHRP) and the Code of Federal Regulations (CRF) require certain information to be provided to individuals before they participate in a research study or activity and Sections 3.10, 8.02 and 8.04 of the American Psychological Association's 'Ethical Principles of Psychologists and Code of Conduct' states that participants who are legally incapable of giving informed consent must still be in receipt of an appropriate explanation. Further, those working with the individual must consider the individuals' preferences and best interests and only obtain appropriate permission from a legally authorized person if such substitute consent is permitted or required by law (for more information see www.socialpsychology.org/consent.htm//apa). In the UK, the Mental Capacity (England and Wales) Act 2005 and the Adults with Incapacity (Scotland) Act 2000 recognize that adults may be able to make some decisions even if they are not able to consent to other decisions.

Therefore it should not be assumed that people with autism are unable to make their own decisions about participating in activities, even when it may be considered to be in their best interest to do so. Informed consent to participate should always be sought before any activities are begun. The publication *Seeking Consent: Working with People with Learning Disabilities* (Department of Health 2001a) provides help on consent issues, and below we offer some general guidelines to consider when using the worksheets with exercises provided in this book.

- All participants should be able to make an informed choice as to their participation or non-participation in the exercises. In other words, they must have the capacity (competency) to consent.

- For individuals to have the capacity to make a decision and consent to an activity, they must possess an understanding of the basic information required to carry out the activity; they must be able to retain this information; and use it to make a choice as to whether or not they begin and continue with the activity (Mental Capacity Act 2005).

- Individuals must be given enough information in order to make a decision about whether to participate in an exercise in this book or not. The information needs to be appropriate and in an accessible format to enable the individual to understand it.

- Assessment of an individual's capacity to consent must not be affected or compromised by organizational factors (e.g. time pressures) or the personal opinion of the assessor as to either the ability of the individual to make a decision or the 'reasonableness' of their decision. This latter point refers to where an assessor finds a decision irrational because it is based on the individual's own religious belief or value system. However, the person with autism is entitled to make their decision for whatever reason they choose. Assessment of capacity to consent should therefore be made using by a professional objective judgement given that the person will be assisted to make their own decisions where possible (Department of Health 2001a).

- If there is doubt concerning informed consent, advice should be sought from a range of people including family members, carers, staff or friends of the individual with autism.

- Individuals should be able to communicate their decision to consent to engage in the exercises. This can be done either by written or oral (taped) agreement, or by using other appropriate communication aids (e.g. signs, symbols, pictures).

- Participation in any activity must be voluntary on the part of the individual with autism – they must not be put under duress to engage in the exercises in this book.

- Even where individuals have given their consent, they should be provided with the opportunity to 'back out' of starting any exercise.

- Some individuals may feel happy to participate on a particular day, but not on another. Where this is the case, it should be reiterated to them that they can participate as and when they feel they wish to.

- In summary, seeking consent should be seen by staff/carers as a process, not a one-off event (Department of Health 2001a) and every effort should be made to ensure that the person with autism (a) knows what they are letting themselves in for, (b) makes a clear decision whether or not to take part, and (c) has their decision respected by those supporting them.

We have provided the following list of questions (based on an idea by Morris, Niederbuhl and Mahr 1993 and Arscott, Dagnan and Kroese 1998) which might also be useful to check the person's level of understanding. However, please note that these questions were originally intended to be used with a series of vignettes (short stories) describing individuals being offered treatments requiring informed consent. They were also intended to be used with a scoring system (a score of 1 indicating understanding, a score of 0 indicating a lack of understanding). However, we would not wish for low scores to result in a person not having their loss addressed. Therefore we suggest they are used only as a guide.

- What will I talk to you about/do with you?

- How long will I talk to you/do the activity with you?

- Are there good things about talking to/doing the activity with me?

- What are these good things?

- Are there bad things about talking to/doing the activity with me?

- What are these bad things?

- What will you do if you don't want to talk to/do activities with me any more?

- What will you do if you have any questions about what we have talked about/the activities?

- Will I tell other people about the things you have told me?

- Are you happy to carry on talking to me/doing the activity?

Observation of an individual may reveal that whilst they initially gave their consent to participate in activities, their behaviour partway through the tasks suggests they have withdrawn consent even though they have not said so. We advise that during activities participants are continually asked if they wish to carry on or take a break, or told that they can stop at any time so that they are engaging on a voluntary basis.

Once the session/activity has been completed we suggest that the facilitator supports the person to evaluate the session (using the Feedback Form on p.53). Concrete arrangements for follow-up should be made, advice on further information provided and if necessary referral to a professional for psychological guidance should be given.

Most ethics committees (including the UK National Research Ethics Service which co-ordinates the Central Office of Research Ethics Committees (see www.nres.npsa.nhs.uk /applicants/index.htm) and the Tizard Centre Ethics Committee, University of Kent, Canterbury) now require those proposing to conduct research or interventions on vulnerable people to address ethical principles. In addition to the issues around consent already discussed, we provide a checklist of ethical values (see Fact Sheet 1.2) which we think are worth considering before you engage in supporting someone with autism to do our exercises. You may wish to photocopy these, laminate them and display them somewhere where they will remind you of what to think about each time you want to use one of the worksheets. You should be able to talk through these values with the person with autism depending on their capabilities so that they are also aware of your responsibilities to them.

Getting started

The worksheets may be used in part or in entirety. Sessions can be conducted daily or weekly with homework in between. Before starting the sessions, the person supporting the individual with autism should talk to them about their particular loss to check shared understanding of it. We give some general guidelines below about how to do this (and how not to do this).

THINGS TO DO WHEN TALKING ABOUT A LOSS WITH SOMEONE WITH AUTISM

- Sit alongside rather than directly opposite to help reduce power imbalances.
- Sit at the same eye level.
- Speak at a similar speed to which the person speaks.
- Tell the person they will be listened to.
- Allow the person to ask questions.
- Answer questions immediately.
- Accept answers given.
- Accept their feelings.
- If you don't know the answer, say so.
- Allow sufficient silence to enable the expression of feelings.
- Check back with the person that you understand what they said by reporting it to them in a different way.

THINGS TO SAY WHEN TALKING ABOUT A LOSS WITH SOMEONE WITH AUTISM

- 'Other people feel the same way.'
- 'Your feelings are normal.'
- 'I know that you feel sad, angry, lonely…etc.'
- Respond to comments by saying, 'Ah ha, uh hum, yes, right, I understand.'
- Conversations need to have a clear structure, be focused and directed towards a definite goal, conducted according to a set plan, e.g. 'We will talk about that later, we have to finish this first' or 'I will take note of it and we'll come back to it next time.'

Things *not* to do

- Keep asking, 'Do you understand?'
- Ask multiple questions.
- Interrupt when they are talking about their experience.
- Ask closed questions.
- Say, 'You'll get over it in time.'
- Say, 'Don't cry' or 'Don't be angry.'
- Say, 'I know how you feel.'

HOW LONG SHOULD YOU SPEND ON EACH WORKSHEET?

Each worksheet should take as long as is appropriate for the developmental level of the particular person. It might be useful to start with ten minutes and gradually increase the duration and frequency of sessions. It is important not to make the sessions too long and we advise no longer than 60 minutes. The tasks should be broken up and there should be at least one complete break. The person with autism should be told from the outset the timing of the sessions, their start and end time, and the number of breaks.

WORKING THROUGH THE ACTIVITIES

All activities should be as concrete as possible by illustrating everything with examples relevant to the person's everyday life. Use simple drawings or any other visual means (see section on Somerset Total Communication, p.28). Activities should not be patronizing in any way. You will need to guard against providing too much information since this can lead to concerns remaining undisclosed or unresolved. Special attention should be paid to fears or bizarre fantasies aroused by the subject. Give the person with autism enough time to ask questions and make remarks. People with autism are very keen on classifying, labelling and listing things, so get them to write, draw and fill things in as much as possible.

WHO SHOULD SUPPORT THE PERSON WITH AUTISM?

Whilst an independent person can provide support unsullied by any previous negative experiences, we recognize that this is not always possible within services, especially those strapped for resources. Therefore we would recommend the following:

- The supporter should be someone other than a person's key worker so that (a) some objectivity can be brought to the working relationship, and (b) it increases the amount of individual support received.

- Time should be set aside to discuss with someone who knows the person well to ascertain the participant's communication skills as well as the types of information and approach/interactional styles they respond to best.

- The supporter must have a positive attitude and empowering style as well as a good sense of humour.

- Time also needs to be set aside for mutual trust to be found between the person with autism and their supporter for ease of expressing feelings.

WHERE SHOULD THE ACTIVITY TAKE PLACE?

Ideally the person with autism should choose the room where the activities will take place so that they feel as comfortable as possible. It is best if the sessions are always held in the same room and that breaks are always taken in another room. Attention needs to be paid to lighting and appropriate furniture (e.g. a table may be needed) as well as the likelihood of disturbances by other people or noise. People with autism should be enabled to be in control of their own surroundings and supported to feel relaxed.

The activities may evoke some negative feelings that the person with autism may find difficult to express appropriately. You should make sure that both yourself and the person with autism can leave the room quickly and easily and that there is someone else close to hand who could assist if required.

Group work

Working through the tasks within a group can be advantageous since they show people with autism that:

- other people with autism suffer the same sorts of responses to loss as they do

- loss can be experienced in different ways for different people

- everyone has different ways of coping with the difficulties of loss.

Group work is also useful since:

- it is sometimes less threatening than one-to-one work

- people with autism may accept statements and suggestions from other group members which they might not take from a carer

- it encourages sharing of experiences, listening to each other, learning and curiosity, the sense of 'community' being a form of support in itself.

However, there are disadvantages to group work, including the following:

- Participants may think they are coping well compared to other group members. Whilst this may be good for self-esteem it might also lead to denial of difficulties and refusal of more support.

- Arguments may arise, especially between people who have shared negative histories.

- Dominant members might monopolize the group, leading to non-participation of others.

- There may be fewer opportunities for individualizing and adapting the exercises to each person.

- People with communication difficulties might find it harder to listen or speak in a group, especially if the group is ill-managed and everyone is talking at once.

- People need courage to say things in front of a group.

If group work is the only option, then ground rules about turn taking, listening to one another and not interrupting will need to be spelt out at the start of the sessions.

General considerations when using the worksheets

As stated, we do not wish to provide a professionalized list of ways of working with people with autism which would fail to be person-centred. However, given the ethical issues discussed above, we have devised a protocol (see Fact Sheet 1.3) as a guide to help ease the people you are working with into the tasks, and to help you think about what their specific needs might be. Such protocols have been used successfully within research before (see Bloom 2005; Cambridge and Forrester-Jones 2003; Long 2005) and we strongly recommend the use of ours before each exercise begins. Similar to the fact sheet, this protocol may be laminated and placed somewhere where you can readily view it.

We also provide a general introductory worksheet (Worksheet 1.1) with two exercises called 'Getting to know you' and 'The story of my loss' to be used at the start of the sessions and an evaluation/feedback form which can be used after each session. The evaluation form should enable you to gauge the extent to which the person with autism is comfortable with the level and format of the exercises and whether they wish to continue with any other activities provided in the book.

Fact Sheet 1.1

The basics of loss and autism

This book is about how people with autism experience different types of loss in their lives. We will look at loss of the following:

relationships

home and possessions

role (e.g. being a child

worker

girl/boyfriend)

health

and feeling well

death

Autism and ASC

If you have autism you may experience loss in a different way to people without autism (neuro-typical people or NTs). Autism or autistic spectrum condition (ASC) refers to a condition which is caused by a hereditary disorder of the brain or problems at birth or birth damage or disease.[1]

If you are autistic your brain works but in a different way to NTs.

You receive and process information differently from NTs and at a slower speed.

For example, you may be mono-tracked. This means you can only process one bit of information at a time and may miss information; struggle to listen and look at the same time; be unable to interpret the body language and facial expressions of another person whilst they are talking to you. You may sometimes experience difficulties in doing some activities.

You may also have difficulties with your senses.

You may hear and smell things that other people don't. This can be useful but also distracting.

---

1 Frith, U. (1989) *Autism: Explaining the Enigma.* Oxford: Blackwell; Frith, U. (1991) *Autism and Asperger Syndrome.* Cambridge: Cambridge University Press.

For example, if a fridge is humming, it will seem so loud to you that you may find you cannot concentrate on doing anything else.

Or music which does not sound loud to others may sound too loud for you.

All of these difficulties may result in impairments or behaviours which can be challenging.

For example, you may find it difficult to communicate with other people.

The anxiety of only being able to focus on one thing at a time might result in obsessions, compulsions and rituals.

Obsessions (e.g. engaging in hobbies) and compulsions (e.g. washing hands) may relieve stress and anxiety whilst rituals (e.g. engaging in routines) are used to relieve the strain of

information processing. People may engage in these behaviours

prior to as well as *during* and *after* doing something they think might be

stressful.

Similarly,

people with autism look and sound the same as NTs. But their behaviour is often misunderstood by those around them as being 'odd'.

Because of this, people with autism are often rejected by their peers and can be lonely.

People with autism and loss

Before the 1960s people didn't really talk about loss or death. Then new theories came along[2] which helped us understand what it is like to lose something and the different stages we go through when we are upset about losing something.

These stages include:

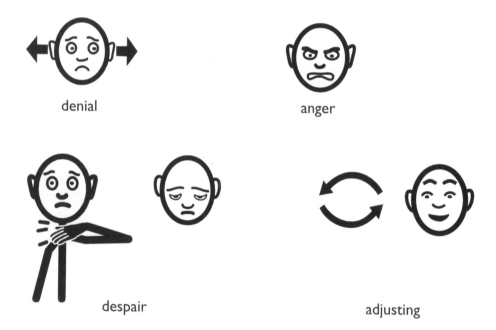

denial

anger

despair

adjusting

People don't always go through every one of these stages, but they are all interrelated. If you have autism, you may also go through these stages but the feelings, thoughts and behaviours you show may be intensified, misunderstood and not dealt with because of the underlying problems you experience of having autism. If no one helps you with your loss, then you may start to become very anxious, behave in a challenging way and become depressed. The exercises in this book are designed to help people with autism move through their loss.

---

2   Like those of Kübler-Ross, E. (1970) *On Death and Dying*. London: Tavistock Routledge; Worden, W.J. (1991) *Grief Counselling and Grief Therapy: A Handbook for the Mental Health Practitioner* (2nd edition). New York: Springer; Stroeke, M. and Schut, H. (1999) 'The dual process model of coping with bereavement: Rationale and description.' *Death Studies 23*, 197–224; and Long, R. (2005) *Loss and Separation*. London: David Fulton Publishers.

Fact Sheet 1.2

Checklist of ethical values

Non-harm: I/we have a duty not to cause harm to any individual participating in the exercises/activities.

Some individuals might become distressed and show challenging behaviour.

In this case a risk assessment might be useful.

However, such an assessment should not lead to delay or work not being undertaken which would further disable service users. Some people may not wish to answer particular questions or engage in discussions about for example:

their social relationships, stigma they might feel, or about the death of a loved one.

Respect for participants' feelings, assurance of confidentiality, the option of stopping or opting out and a complaint system may minimize this risk.

Benefit: I/we have a duty to do good to everyone!

The benefits of the activities to the person with autism should be outlined.

Autonomy: I/we have a duty to help the person to make his/her own decisions.

Consent to participate in exercises/activities should be sought by written or verbal agreement a number of times during the sessions. It should be made clear to individuals that they can stop participating at any time.

Respect for persons: I/we have a duty to value each person and honour their rights and their responsibilities. I/we must not treat anyone as a mere means to my/our end.

Justice: I/we have a duty to treat each person equally and tell the person about any possible risks and benefits of participation in activities…

equally

Confidentiality: I/we have a duty not to tell other people things that are private.

Understanding/Tolerance: I/we have a duty to accept other viewpoints.

Honesty: I/we have a duty always to tell the truth about why we are doing the activities.

Cultural issues: It is possible that some people with autism will be of different cultural and ethnic backgrounds. I/we will be sensitive to their particular needs.

For example, it may be necessary to ask a question in a different and more appropriate format recognizable to people from different cultures, or change an activity to suit particular religious backgrounds. More time might be needed for activities where English is not the first language of participants. Where appropriate, the consultation of a translator should be sought.

Fact Sheet 1.3
Protocol

1. **Seek the person's consent to participate in the activities**.

2. **Know the person**.

Apart from your own knowledge and observation of the person, the advice of a multi-disciplinary team may be helpful. Carers can also provide concrete examples of the types of impairments the person may have.

You will need to know/learn the following information about the person, and may be able to get this via person-centred planning:

    (a) communication level and resource needs

(e.g. materials in different formats such as signs, symbols or photographs)

(b) skills and abilities to participate in exercises

(c) particular personality traits

(d) needs associated with cultural and ethnic background.

3. **Adapt particular worksheets according to the information above**.

4. **Find a comfortable and appropriate (quiet) room/place in which to do the activities**.

5. **Find a room/place in which to take breaks from the exercises**.

6. **Check understanding and repeat information to aid understanding**.

7. **Let the person set his/her own pace for working through the exercises**.

Activities should not be worked through all in one go – following person-centred planning and active support models will help.[3]

8. **End each session on a positive note**.

Treat them to a snack, drink or game, or chat about their favourite subject

---

3   Ashman, B. and Beadle-Brown, J. (2006) *A Valued Life: Developing Person-centred Approaches so People Can Be More Included*. London: United Response; Mansell, J., Beadle-Brown, J., Ashman, B. and Ockendon, J. (2005) *Person-centred Active Support: A Multi-media Training Resource for Staff to Enable Participation, Inclusion and Choice for People with Learning Disabilities*. Brighton: Pavilion.

Worksheet 1.1
Getting to know you

Aim: to provide a 'sentence completion task' about the person.

Objective: to be used as a way of getting to know the person better and to help them relax.

We have included two very similar sentences which can be used to check the person's general comprehension. If the person completes both sentences with the same ending, it is a sign that they have understood the statements.

Exercise: Getting to know you

This exercise is called 'Getting to know you'. I am interested in what you do during the day, the things you like and the things you don't like.

Please complete the following sentences:

One thing I like about myself is…

My friends like me because…

I liked it when I did…

My favourite activity is…

I have skills in…

I eat at…(time)

and my favourite meal is…

My favourite food is…

I like doing…

Worksheet 1.2

The story of my loss

Aim: to ask the person to draw the story of what they have lost (does not have to be most recent loss) and to talk about their feelings.

Objective: to help ascertain which loss you will be working with specifically, and to help them begin to talk about their feelings.

Exercise: The story of my loss

Ask the person to draw their story – they can draw the thing/person they have lost.

Use happy, sad and angry faces provided below to help talk about feelings (a sand tray might help to draw these faces).

Use diaries or video diaries (sometimes it can be easier for someone with autism to talk to a video camera than to a person).

Worksheet 1.3
Feedback form

Aim: to find out if the person enjoyed the exercises and whether or not they found them useful/helpful.

Objective: to note issues (e.g. what was helpful/unhelpful; problems encountered in communication and understanding; any adverse effects the exercises have on the person with autism) arising from the exercises and to make any necessary changes to other exercises.

Exercise: Feedback form

Title of exercise

Date of exercise

Please circle your answers

Did you like this exercise? Yes No Don't know

Was this exercise good? Yes No Don't know

Or was this exercise bad? Yes No Don't know

Why was it good/bad?

Draw or write your answer here

Did the exercise help you?

Yes

No

Don't know

How did the exercise help you/not help you?

Draw or write your answer here

Is there anything else you want to say/tell me about the exercise?

Draw or write your answer here

How can we make the exercise better?

Draw or write your answer here

Chapter 2

Loss of Social Relationships

No man is an Island, entire of itself;…any man's death diminishes me, because I am involved in Mankind; And therefore never send to know for whom the bell tolls; It tolls for thee.

John Donne, Meditation XVII,
Devotions upon Emergent Occasions (1624)

Introduction

It is a truth universally acknowledged that we all need friends, social contacts and relationships in order to feel socially included within our communities (Forrester-Jones and Grant 1997). Belonging to a social network potentially allows us to access companionship, laughter, adventure, advice and guidance as well as practical and emotional support, including love and affection (McConkey 2005).

Why are social networks worth having?

Research concerning a range of client groups both in the UK and the USA has shown that social relationships which provide social support are associated with:

- maintenance of individual health and personal wellbeing (Eurelings-Bontekoe, Diestra and Verschuur 1995)

- buffering stress (Cassel 1976; Lin and Dean 1985)

- recovery from mental ill health (Wall 1998)

- happiness (Chadsey and Beyer 2001)

- self-esteem and confidence (Srivastava 2001).

Social networks can also be associated with secondary outcomes such as:

- participation in leisure activities (Forrester-Jones 2001)

- gaining and securing employment (Strathdee 2005)

- access to other services (Wayslenki *et al.* 1993)

- greater personal freedom or autonomy (O'Brien 1987).

The quality of our lives then is determined by the range and type of social relationships we have (Cummins and Lau 2003). 'Social network members' may provide informal social support (e.g. family, friends, neighbours) or more formal support (e.g. paid carers, professionals, work colleagues, teachers). A social network made up of a range of different types of relationships, including weak ties (Grannoveter 1995) (e.g. swimming instructor, taxi driver, retailer) and stronger ties (e.g. parent, or friend acting as a confidante), also places fewer demands on staff support. However, a network of relationships may provide little or no social support (Forrester-Jones *et al.* 2006) or the support provided might provoke stress, be construed by the person receiving it as unhelpful (Rook 1992) or abusive (Cambridge 1999). A social network may therefore be regarded as an 'opportunity structure' (Forrester-Jones and Grant 1997) which plays a critical role in determining which resources, if any, are accessed (see Figure 2.1).

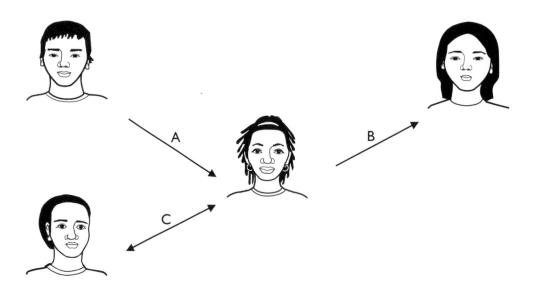

Figure 2.1 Social network showing (A) support received, (B) support provided and (C) support reciprocated

Social network structure

Network structure refers not only to network membership but also to the size and density of the network, and the areas of life from which network members come. We describe these, together with frequency and duration of interaction, below.

SIZE

Social networks vary in size (i.e. the number of relationships attached to the person). Networks may be large (e.g. populations studies in the US by Sarason *et al.* (1983) reported an average network size of over 100 persons); or small (e.g. Forrester-Jones *et al.* 2006) reported an average network size of 22 for people with learning disabilities across England). Whilst having a large number of network members does not necessarily equate with getting a large amount of support, opportunities for social inclusion are increased with more network members. Restricted social networks are linked to behavioural and mental health problems (Raitasuo, Virtanen and Raitasuo 1998) as well as communication difficulties (Cambridge and Forrester-Jones 2003).

DENSITY

Density refers to the proportion of network members who know each other. A high-density network means that most or all network members know each other. Burt (1997) argues that such networks can provide 'social capital', or opportunities for social support, since people within groups circulate information between one another. However, individuals who have a high-density network are at risk of being socially segregated, experiencing restricted outlooks/horizons, lack of privacy and possible exploitation. Conversely, a low-density network comprising clusters of members who do not know each other may allow more scope for new experiences and relationships, and less chance for powerful individuals to exert influence over others.

AREA OF LIFE

Referring to the social context of network members (e.g. family, school work), studies of the social networks of people with learning disabilities have shown that the majority of network members come from areas of life most likely to include other people with learning disabilities (e.g. day centre) (Forrester-Jones *et al.* 2004). However, there has been virtually no research investigating where people with autism derive their social contacts from.

FREQUENCY AND DURATION OF CONTACT

How often individuals have contact with network members (e.g. daily, weekly, monthly or yearly) and how long the relationships have lasted can tell us much about the quality of the network. Bauminger and Shulman (2003) argue that friendship is based on reciprocal and stable social interactions (e.g. six months or more). However, in their study of mothers' perceptions of friendships they found that children with autism met their friends less often and that these friendships were less stable (shorter duration) compared to their NT counterparts.

Social relationships and people with autism

Developing and maintaining social networks

Research studies of people with learning disabilities (including autism) have shown that living in community-based residential services has generally resulted in larger, more diverse social networks than people experienced in segregated institutional care (e.g. Robertson *et al.* 2001; O'Callaghan and Murphy 2002; Hatzidimitriadou and Forrester-Jones 2002; Forrester-Jones *et al.* 2004; Heller 2002; Forrester-Jones *et al.* 2006). However, the American Association on Intellectual and Developmental Disabilities (AAIDD) states that person-centred planning requires building both personal and community support (AAIDD 2007), and present UK government policy states that 'helping people sustain friendships is consistently shown as being one of the greatest challenges faced by learning disability services' (DoH 2001b, para 7.39).

Indeed, the lack of, and need for, friendship, especially during evenings and weekends, seems to be an issue for many people with learning disabilities, including those with autism living independently or with family in the community (Schwabenland 1999; St Quintin and Disney 2003). Bauminger and Kasari (2000) and Jones and Meldal (2001) found a significantly higher incidence of reported loneliness and desire for friends amongst children with autism compared to neuro-typical (NT) children, and Stoddart (1999) argues that adolescence is particularly challenging for people with autism who wish for intimate relationships. In a study of regular classroom inclusiveness, Chamberlain, Kasari and Rotheram-Fuller (2007) found that children with autism reported involvement in networks but experienced little acceptance, companionship and reciprocity from network relationships, though they did not report greater loneliness than their NT counterparts. Chamberlain *et al.* argue that further work is needed to help children with autism move from the periphery to more effective engagement with their peers.

Networks of people with autism can also appear to be segregated and transient in nature, with members (especially paid carers) entering and leaving individuals' lives on a regular basis. This is not unusual in itself (many of us experience 'fair weather friends' or social acquaintances who come and go). However, when a person's social network is already small, the *loss* of a member will be particularly difficult to bear. Similarly, people may feel that they have 'lost out' if their wish for an intimate relationship or for children does not materialize (McCarthy 1999).

Figure 2.2 shows the social network of a NT person, Figure 2.3 the network of a person with autism. Note the stark differences between the two networks. In Figure 2.2 we see that the person has ten different areas of life from which to draw network members from. Some of these clusters of people are connected to other clusters (e.g. family members are connected to five other clusters of people including old school friends, neighbours, ski holidays, church and tennis club). However, six clusters of network members are connected to only one other cluster and one cluster is a 'stand-alone' cluster. On the other hand, Figure 2.3 shows the person with autism only having four different areas of life to which all network members are connected. For this person, there is the potential that the network is too high in density.

Issues related to autism

There is a wide range of reasons why people on the autistic spectrum struggle to develop and maintain social networks, although the research into this area has so far been limited

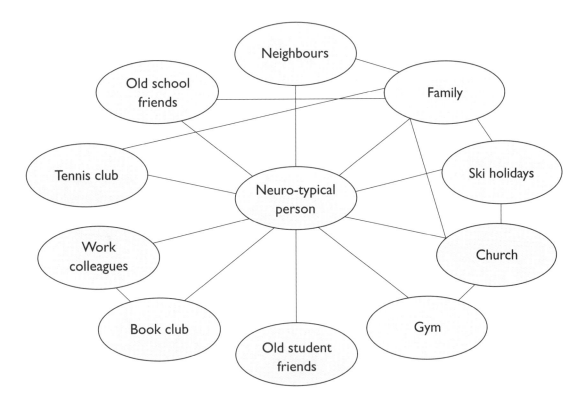

Figure 2.2 The social network of a neuro-typical person

(Howard, Cohn and Orsmond 2006). In the introductory chapter of this resource we outlined some of the main difficulties people with autism have; below we shall see how these difficulties as well as others impact on their social relationships including losing network members. In so doing we will also dispel some myths about people with autistic spectrum condition (ASC).

BEING MONO-TRACKED

Socially, this impacts on an individual's ability to hold reciprocal conversations since 'people' are the most multi-sensory objects in our environment, demanding an incredible amount of information-processing. For example, when we talk to someone we look at their facial expression, we hear their voice tone and the words they speak, and at the same time we have a sense of ourselves. This is discussed further in Chapter 1.

A person with ASC may have difficulties processing all of this information simultaneously and be unable to experience how their own behaviour (i.e. what they say or do) might impact on the other person's feelings. These problems may account for what is termed in the US as 'limited joint attention skills' (Travis and Sigman 1998) and 'deficient theory of mind' (Leslie 1987; Leslie and Roth 1993), or for the inability of a person with ASC to understand that others have different thoughts, desires and views to themselves. Leekam *et al.* (1997) argue that adolescents and adults with autism may have well-developed joint attention capabilities but fail to display them in the appropriate circumstances. Interaction may therefore be problematic and lead to misunderstandings.

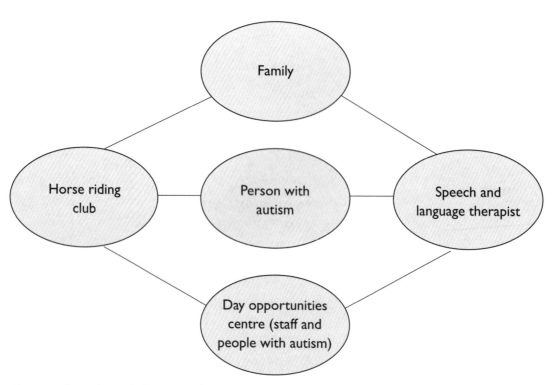

Figure 2.3 The social network of a person with autism

For example, people may feel that their interaction with a person with autism is not recip-rocated and so will move on, seeking friendship elsewhere, the person with autism losing out (Clements 2005).

Whilst it is a *myth* that people with autism *consciously* avoid eye contact or are *unable to empathize* with others, their difficulties in processing lots of information means that they may be unable to respond quickly enough or provide the verbal and non-verbal cues (e.g. smile or use brief verbal responses like 'OK' or 'right') to indicate empathy (Cesaroni and Garber 1991) or to encourage the other person to continue dialogue (Hobson and Lee 1998). They may also have difficulty in processing teasing or irony (Attwood 2006) and be less likely to turn spontaneously to look in the same direction as another person is looking and comment on what is being seen at the same time. To counteract the problem of being mono-tracked some individuals may try to keep one sense 'on-line' by repetitive behaviour such as tapping, whilst tuning into another sense. Alternatively, they may try to tune in completely to everything around them but will end up overloading and shutting down (Williams 2006). These behaviours will impact on the development of relationships. A prospective friend who does not understand such difficulties may interpret the behaviour as rude or odd, ruling the person with ASC out of their social network. It is little wonder that mothers have reported that their children with autism have difficulties initiat-ing and sustaining friendships (Bauminger and Shulman 2003).

STRUGGLING WITH ORGANIZATIONAL AND PROBLEM-SOLVING SKILLS

People with these difficulties are unable easily to adapt to changed circumstances. Whenever they perform tasks which are slightly different from what they were previously (e.g. using public transport, shopping, eating out at a different restaurant or different table in the same restaurant), they will find it difficult to work out how to adapt their behaviour to the situation. This means that leisure activities which are potential routes to 'friend finding', 'friend maturing' and 'friend maintaining' may in fact end up being disastrous for people with ASC unless support is provided to prepare for all possible eventualities. People with ASC may quickly begin to feel anxious when confronted with new situations leading to repetitive/ritualistic or obsessive/compulsive behaviour. This may calm their anxiety, but may be regarded as socially unacceptable, embarrassing or challenging to others in the group. Unable to cope with this behaviour, the group may struggle to include the person with ASC in similar activities, and the person with ASC may not wish to repeat what is perceived as a bad experience. Rather, they wish to revert to familiar routines and in the process get 'left out' of and lose the social network. When this happens it is a real loss, since it is a *myth* that people with autism do not want friends or to belong to communities (Hurlbutt and Chalmers 2002). It is also a *myth* that they are 'loners' or don't want to join in and do things such as talking and playing with other people.

SOCIAL SKILLS

We need social intelligence for social interaction to take place successfully especially with people we have only just met. This means that we need to be skilled at learning and assessing what the other person responds to and to adapt our behaviour accordingly. People with ASC may have been taught social skills and be able to use them. However, social competence needs multiple social skills. For example, a successful verbal greeting of 'hello' also needs to encompass a smile and eye contact. Since people with ASC are mono-tracked (see above), then putting these three components together can be tricky (Mitchell 2005). Lawson (2001, p.16), giving a personal account of living with ASC, stated: 'I lacked social skills and the "know how" of friendship building.' Similarly Mitchell (2005, p.47), recounting his student days, stated: 'Very quickly, I was beginning to feel out of place at journalism school, not just in terms of being a slow developer, but also in terms of how under-developed my social skills were.' This may be one of the reasons for the decline in interest in social skills training, since individual components of social skills (e.g. manners of saying 'thank you' when passed a plate of sandwiches) taught to a person are not always convincingly absorbed into a seamless repertoire of social graces (e.g. smiling, saying thank you and passing the plate of sandwiches on to the next person). Further, research has shown that social skills training may be successful within the context of which it is taught, but there are few studies that indicate whether such training generalizes to social interactions in the community (Dilk and Bond 1996).

Whilst social skills are necessary for friendship to develop and be maintained, friendship also enables people to practise these skills (Bauminger and Shulman 2003). Unfortunately, many people with autism find themselves locked in a never-ending circle of having few friends to practise their social skills on, leading to a lack of developed social skills, resulting in a shortage of new activities and experiences which friends might bring along. This means that people with ASC are left with a short supply of things to talk about other than something connected to services. They end up being trapped in service-bound social contexts. Others may suffer from inflexibility of thought (see Table 1.1) with social conversations tending to centre around particular subjects. Sometimes the topic areas are inappropriate for the social context (e.g. talking about sexual needs or wants on a first encounter with someone). Such 'odd' conversations can lead potential network members to label people with ASC as eccentric or strange. Heightened arousal by social encounters that need abilities in conflict resolution and compromise (Newcomb and Bagwell 1996) result in defensive strategies such as social withdrawal (Tarrier *et al.* 1979).

SENSORY DIFFICULTIES

People with ASC sometimes find close proximity to others or touch to be unpleasant or stressful, which can cause difficulties, especially when relationships begin to become intimate. Mitchell (2005, p.42) recounts how he felt awkward and immature even talking about intimate relationships, stating: 'I couldn't and still often don't understand how such relationships form.' The person with autism experiencing touch may back off or show dis-comfort, which can be interpreted by the significant other as a sign of dislike. Kanner (1943) proposed that such behaviour indicated that children with autism were indifferent to their parents. However, this has now been debunked as a *myth* as studies comparing at-tachment behaviours in children with autism to those without have consistently found no evidence to support this claim. Rather, some people with autism may have difficulties in appreciating the personal spaces of others, standing so close to the extent that their breath is felt on the other person's neck (leading to feelings of confusion, anxiety and possible rejection by the other person).

Some people with ASC find certain clothes more comfortable to wear than others. These preferred clothes might be very unfashionable. Whilst this should/does not matter to the vast majority of people, it often matters to teenagers and for those individuals with autism who wish to belong to the peer group or 'gang of friends', this issue can add stress to an already tenuous level of acceptance.

Environmental issues

- *Location*: Some people with autism live in isolated geographical areas for most of their lives. Their life trajectories have often prevented opportunities to add or replace lost network members based on family, home and school with new ones based on work, interests and friendship (Tyne 1989). Rather, they have lived with or in close proximity to staff and other 'service users' for many years, sometimes since childhood.

- *Inappropriate or unavailable transport* can act as a barrier stopping people with autism experiencing many community activities. This is illustrated in the case study of Claire in Chapter 5 who is unable to attend her local church where she knows many people, because staff are unavailable to take her there on Sundays.

- *Staffing level, regimes and culture* might curtail the development of relationships and contribute to their loss. First, staff who feel overburdened and pressured by time or who are concerned about professional boundaries tend to adopt relationships with service users characterized by formal instructional interaction (Forrester-Jones *et al.* 2002). However, Mansell and Beadle-Brown (2004) argue that staff numbers are not as important to successful services as good care practices (the pattern and nature of interaction and support directly provided by staff to the people they serve). Second, paternalistic attitudes by staff including a fear of people with ASC 'choosing the wrong friends' or 'making a mistake' (Downer 2000) might restrict people with ASC from developing friendships and relationships. The risk of a person with autism 'being taken advantage of' or 'being hurt' or abused by others who misinterpret their friendly behaviour and do not reciprocate it in the same way can be too great a burden to bear for some staff (Melberg Schwier and Hingsburger 2000) as well as families who feel responsible for the person in their care. Staff need to be trained and encouraged to worry less about potential mistakes people with ASC may make with relationships whilst at the same time managing real risks.

The following case study of Geoff illustrates many of the issues above:

Case study – Geoff

Geoff, who is 35 and has autism and a mild learning disability, has lived in a residential care home for four people (the others all have moderate to severe learning disabilities) for the last five years. The home is situated in a small village on a steep hill in North Wales. Previously Geoff lived with his parents in a larger town in the valley but when his parents died, Geoff had no other relatives in the area and the care home was his only option. There is little to do in the village and it is difficult to go anywhere on public transport, especially at night as taxis are expensive. Consequently Geoff does not get out much and doesn't know many people apart from those in his residence. He gets on 'OK' with them but he wouldn't call them his friends. This has caused some consternation as Geoff used to belong to a couple of daytime and evening clubs when he lived with his parents. However, he has not been able to attend these due to transport and staffing issues. The service is trying to sort something out for Geoff but it has been a long time since he has seen the few friends he has.

Geoff has therefore recently lost not only the companionship of his parents but also other friends and staff in addition to his home. Llewellyn and McConnell (2002) suggest that people living with parents invariably means they have smaller networks almost entirely made up of family members compared with those living in community houses. However, Geoff's story shows that networks can be depleted once the parental home is lost. It has also been shown that families with a member who has autism may find their networks shrink progressively over time (Whitman 2004). NT siblings may respond to the disability by distancing themselves as far as possible from their brother or sister, moving away from home as soon as they can, and even denying that their sibling exists. It is not uncommon to find a middle-aged person with ASC being cared for by elderly parents, with no other relatives in touch. This isolation is intensified if parents are over-involved with their son or daughter, maintaining an exclusive relationship with him/her. Geoff's story also reflects what Schwabenland (1999) argued, that placement's success depends on the mix of people (including age, gender and personality) in a community house.

Outcomes of relationship loss for people with autism

There are virtually no specific research studies about the impact of losing relationships on people with autism. Rather, studies about autism tend to repeat the fact that the basic building blocks for interpersonal relationships are impaired. The loss or breakdown of a friendship, parental marital breakdown or even the loss of a family pet can have a devastating impact on a person with autism. Many people on the autistic spectrum suffer with poor self-esteem (see Chapter 5 'Loss of Health and Wellbeing') and the loss of a friendship can cause further damage to their sense of self. They may feel even more different if, having lost a friend who also has autism, they find themselves amongst NTs and on the receiving end of teasing or rejection (Attwood 2006; Lawson 2003). As mentioned above, this can be particularly difficult during adolescence, when friendships are beginning to become more intimate, both emotionally and physically (Howard *et al.* 2006). Loss of such a relationship can leave a person with autism feeling angry and confused, particularly if the friendship has ended suddenly or without explanation. If the friend had a certain role or was responsible for doing specific things with or for the person with autism, they may become anxious about who is going to do those things now that the friend has gone. Such emotions can lead to either the beginnings of, or an increase in, aggressive behaviour towards others (e.g. sexualizing and verbal abuse, biting, kicking, hitting, using weapons) or self-injurious behaviour (e.g. striking their head against a solid surface, running out into a busy road with seemingly no safety awareness, eating harmful substances) and obsessive/ritualistic behaviours. These outcomes are directly related to the problems of being mono-tracked, i.e. not being able to process the actual experience of the loss and the emotions that go with it at the same time. Cause and effect are not always linked. For example, if a person with autism loses someone special in their lives, they may not respond to this emotionally until some time after the event, at which time they are unable to make the connection between their feelings and emotions with the loss. The behaviours that result from this can be difficult to manage, especially when the lost relationship is with a person such as a key worker who generally helped them with behavioural difficulties such as anxiety or anger management. Alternatively, the person with autism may refuse to do specific activities if the person they used to do those activities with is no longer present. This can have a detrimental effect on the health of the individual and their sense of wellbeing.

How to help people with autism deal with relationship loss

For many people with autism the social world is a puzzling and difficult place (Clements and Zarkowska 2000). Broken relationships can be extremely painful for anyone but for someone with autism subsequent attempts at engaging socially may be fraught with social blunders, misunderstanding and mistakes. A person with autism may replace a lost relationship with sensory pleasure seeking, which may lead to social withdrawal and isolation.

It is therefore very important that whoever is left supporting the individual acknowledges the fact that someone special is no longer a part of their lives and that this must be difficult for them. Acknowledging this can be done by talking through the loss and the emotional response to it as shown in Worksheet 2.1 below. At the same time, people can only feel, function and survive by being part of a wider social supportive group. Worksheet 2.3 below can be used to map and describe the social support network of individuals. It can also be used to show how networks have changed over time and where gaps are in relation to support provided.

When someone with autism loses a social relationship for whatever reason, it is important that others who are part of the person's life maintain and show a positive regard for them through social interactions, comments and behaviour. Since they may have lost an important source of positive support, they will need access to others who will provide day-to-day pleasure, comfort and humour as well as people who can show understanding, empathy and acceptance of their individual difficulties and needs including unexplained emotions. It is unlikely that one person can provide all of these types of support and therefore the person with autism needs to be surrounded by a range of people who will value them.

It may also be necessary to find ways in which the person can withdraw safely from social interaction if they are overwhelmed by it and spend some structured time alone without it becoming a permanent state (Clements and Zarkowska 2000).

Facilitating positive social engagement may be built up gradually by spending 'bite sized' chunks of time with the person, engaging in their preferred activities and listening to their described feelings of loneliness. These times can be built up to longer, structured periods. Maintaining consistency and continuity whilst at the same time offering choices (including the choice to engage or not engage in an activity) will be important during these sessions. Clements (2005) and Clements and Zarkowska (2000) suggest that the supporter needs to have a high level of personal consistency in moods, boundaries and expectations of the person with autism as well as tolerance of their behaviour.

Despite all of the difficulties outlined above, studies show that people with autism including children can and do succeed in maintaining social relationships with their siblings (Knott, Lewis and Williams 1995), parents and NT friends (Bauminger and Kasari 2000). Supporting people with autism to develop relationships is a daunting task. McConkey (2005) argues that whilst support staff can organize common leisure activities, parties and group outings to enable people both to see each other regularly and to learn the necessary communication and social skills needed for conversations (Bigelow and LaGaipa 1975), they cannot force people to make or be friends, since friendship is voluntary by nature (Wenger 1984). Further, there is no prescribed way of helping people make new friends once they have lost some. Attempts to 'match-make' friendships through 'befriending' and 'relationship support' and 'dating agency' services (see Jenner and Gale 2006) have had mixed results. Some friendships form instantaneously from initial introductions; others take a long time to evolve. Some friendships have a lot in common; other friends reflect the old saying 'opposites attract'. Some friendships last a lifetime, whilst others seem to be time and purpose bound. McConkey (2005) also argues that friendship formation is influenced by the prevailing social and cultural attitudes within the communities in which people live including religious affiliation (e.g. Catholics and Protestants, Jews and Muslims, black and fair-skinned people, able and disabled). Nevertheless, it is important that people with autism are supported to maintain the relationships they have and be given the opportunity to make new friends.

The objectives of the exercises are first to enable individuals to express their feelings and emotions in the knowledge that relationship losses are a natural part of life and second, to help look at how individuals may be supported over time to improve their social network or 'opportunity structure' in order to gain social support. Apart from our exercises below, we provide references to resources which we think will be of help in terms of developing social skills, providing opportunities to meet people, and forming and maintaining friendships. These are as follows:

- Gammeltoft, L. and Nordenhof, M.S. (2007) *Autism, Play and Social Interaction.* London: Jessica Kingsley Publishers.

- Gutstein, S.E. and Sheely, R.K. (2002) *Relationship Development Intervention with Children, Adolescents and Adults.* London: Jessica Kingsley Publishers.

- Lawson, W. (2006) *Friendships: The Aspie Way.* London: Jessica Kingsley Publishers.

- Painter, K.K. (2006) *Social Skills Groups for Children and Adolescents with Asperger's Syndrome: A Step-by-Step Program.* London: Jessica Kingsley Publishers.

- Schneider, C.B. (2006) *Acting Antics: A Theatrical Approach to Teaching Social Understanding to Kids and Teens with Asperger Syndrome.* London: Jessica Kingsley Publishers.

Loss of social relationships

If you have autism, there are a wide range of reasons why you might struggle to develop and maintain social networks.

Being mono-tracked: Socially, this will impact on your ability to hold conversations

since people are the most multi-sensory objects in our environment.

People therefore need a lot of information-processing.

You may also struggle with organizational and problem-solving skills

which require thinking about both the 'now' and the 'future'.

Potential leisure activities

that can be:

'friend finding'

'friend maturing' and

'friend maintaining' may in fact end up being

disastrous if you have an ASC unless

support is provided to prepare for all possible eventualities.

You might quickly begin to feel anxious

with new situations e.g. a new person enters your life who you don't know – leading to

repetitive/ritualistic or obsessive/compulsive behaviour which calms your anxiety but which is regarded as socially

unacceptable, embarrassing

or challenging to others in the group.

Despite all of the difficulties outlined above, studies show

that people with autism can and do succeed in gaining

and maintaining social relationships.

Loss of a relationship can leave you feeling

angry, confused and frustrated,

particularly if the friendship has ended suddenly

or without explanation.

If the friend had a certain role (e.g. key worker) or was responsible for doing

specific things with or for you, you may become anxious

about who is going to do those things now that the friend/key worker has gone.

Such emotions can lead to either the beginnings of, or an increase in,

aggressive, self-injurious and obsessive/ritualistic behaviours.

Alternatively you may refuse to do specific activities if the person you used to do those activities with is no longer present.

This can have a bad effect on your health and your sense of wellbeing.

Worksheet 2.1

Life story of our relationship

Aim: By using the open-ended questions below, the idea is to collect the life story of the person who has 'gone' or been 'lost' (including things which the person with autism can associate to the 'lost network member' such as pictures, photographs, tapes or particular songs, videos, etc.). Please note we have left spaces next to each picture for you to place more appropriate symbols, pictures, photographs, etc. should you need them. These items should be placed in a box file. The putting things in the box should be done by the person with autism, supported by a key worker or preferably someone who knew the 'lost' person. The exercise can last for 15 minutes every day for one month.

Objective: Through talking about and looking at (via photos) the network member who is no longer a part of everyday life, the person with autism can 'remember' what they were like and understand that it is OK to lose someone. A further objective is to understand that it is possible to find other people with the same qualities as the person lost. This is not to say that new people have to replace the lost person, rather that it is OK to have a new friend. The same questions should be asked of someone who was not particularly liked.

Exercise: Life story of our relationship

When did person x enter my life?

What was person x's name?

What did they look like?

What do I remember most about person x?

How did they help me?

What didn't they do – 'I wish they had done…'

What did I like about the person?

What didn't I like about the person?

Worksheet 2.2

What happened to the relationship?

Aim: to use the questions in the exercise to draw a flow chart (we give an example below) describing what happened to the person, why they went away, etc.

Objective: to discuss the feelings the person had when they lost their contact and to work through some of these feelings.

Exercise: What happened to the relationship?

Why did person x leave?

Where did they go?

How did I feel when they went?

How do I feel now? Am I sad, happy, crying, upset?

Example of flow chart of what happened to Jean:

Worksheet 2.3
Moving on

Practical strategies for helping an individual regain their sense of control using the Social Network Guide for people with intellectual disabilities, people with mental health difficulties and people with autism. *Please note that some people will need additional assistance when using this exercise.*

Aim: to chart the social network of the person with autism using the Social Network Guide below. This can be done as part of person-centred planning or as a stand-alone exercise.

Objective: to identify the gaps within the individual's social network and to follow this up every six months (or less) to see if the network has changed or improved in both quantity and quality.

The Social Network Guide (SNG)[1] was adapted and further developed from an instrument called The Social Network Map.[2] Our SNG was modified in various ways in order to be more appropriate for using with people with learning disabilities, mental health difficulties and people with autism. The SNG has been used previously to map the social networks of 213 people with learning disabilities who had been living in community housing for 12 years following deinstitutionalization from long-stay hospitals.[3] The authors are still working on a fuller version of the SNG.

The SNG helps to chart individuals' social networks (the number of people, who they are, and what support they provide).

Please note that the SNG is a bit more detailed than most other exercises in this book and all or just parts of the SNG can be used depending on the person being supported and the depth of knowledge about their social network required.

Using the SNG

To use the SNG, first show the individual the diagram entitled 'My Social Network' (p.84). Ask them to fill in each section of the circle with relevant names (or just initials if they don't want to mention full names) of *all* the people they know. We give an example below of Sam's social

1   Forrester-Jones, R. (1998) *Social Networks and Social Support: Development of an Instrument.* Departmental Working Paper, Tizard Centre, Canterbury, University of Kent; Forrester-Jones, R. and Duplock, L. (in progress) The Social Network Guide: An Instrument to Measure and Understand the Social Networks of People with Mental Health Difficulties, People with Learning Disabilities and People with Autism.

2   Developed for their work investigating parental support by Tracy, E.M. (1990) 'Identifying social support resources: At risk families.' *Social Work* 35, 252–258; Tracy, E.M. and Bell, N.A. (1994) 'Social Network Map: Some further refinements on administration.' *Social Work Research 18*, 1, 56–60; Tracey, E.M. and Whittaker, J.K. (1990) 'The Social Network Map: Assessing social support in clinical practice.' *Families in Society 71*, 8, 461–470.

3   Forrester-Jones, R., Cambridge, P., Carpenter, J., Tate, A., Beecham, J., Hallam, A., Knapp, M., Coolen-Schrijner, P. and Wooff, D. (2006) 'The social networks of people with learning disabilities living in the community twelve years after resettling from long-stay hospital.' *Journal of Applied Research in Intellectual Disability 19*, 285–295.

network with the name 'John' written into the section called 'Household'. You may need to prompt the individual in order to complete each section. For example, for the section called 'Household' you could ask 'Who do you live with?' and for the section called 'Work/Day Centre' you could ask 'Who do you see at the day centre?' or 'Who do you work with?'

Sam's Social Network

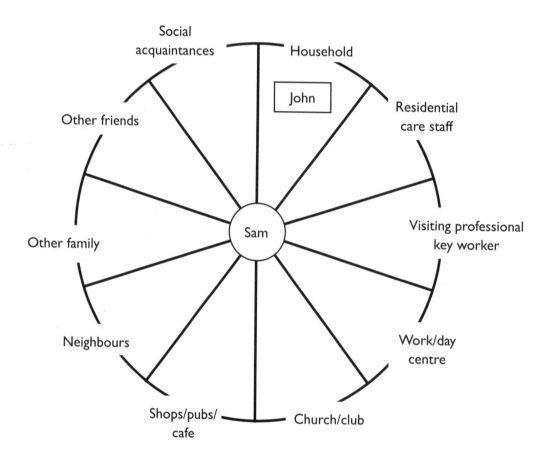

Once completed, 'My Social Network' should have a number of names in each section. Visually you and the person you are supporting will be able to see any gaps in the social network. This may simply be used to investigate where the gaps are and how they might be filled. For example, if the person has no social contacts in the section marked 'Church/Club', then some work might be done in order to seek out if there is an appropriate club the person wishes to attend to meet people. Conversely, if they are already attending a club, the reasons why the person has not met anyone they can name might be investigated.

To explore the individual's social network in a deeper way, take out the 'display sheets' (you can adapt the symbols for your person). The first block (1–11) of symbols on the left hand side of the display sheet shows an array of possible network members which can be pointed to or ticked by the individual using a non-permanent pen and wiped clean each time it is used.

Ask the person you are supporting to describe which membership group each of their named contacts (listed on 'My Social Network') is from. For example, ask the question 'Is John a member of staff, or another service user'? Ask the same questions relating to the block of 1–11 'area of life' options on the right hand side of the display sheet. So, for example, John lives in the same house as Sam and that is how Sam knows him. However, if Sam had met John at the local day centre, then Sam would have ticked 'day centre' in the area of life section in relation to John.

Next, ask your individual with autism about the type of support each network member named provides to them. For example, ask 'Does John help you dress or wash in the morning?' 'Does John help with the cleaning of the house?' Continue asking these questions referring to the eight different types of social support provided on the left hand side of the second display sheet as well as the interactional options/behaviours on the right hand side of the second display sheet. Repeat the steps for every contact shown on 'My Social Network' circle. Please note that the two questions relating to reciprocity are used to check that the client has understood what reciprocity is and to check for acquiescence.

Finally, you can use the scoring sheet provided to total up the number of contacts as well as provide scores for how many of the contacts provide each type of support. For example, 'how many people including John provide Sam with household support?' You can also total up how many contacts Sam sees daily etc.

To fill out the scoring sheet, pick the first name from 'My Social Network' (e.g. in this example it would be John) – John is contact (Cn) number 1. Ask the individual what type of network member (Memb) the contact is and which area of life (AoL) they come from. Mark on the scoring sheet the relevant code number for the response given (each option has a number attached to it, e.g. network member 'staff' will be scored using the code 2 and support behaviour 'decisions' will either be scored 1 or 2.

Analysis

Count up the scores for network membership (e.g. the number of network members in each membership category including 'other service users', 'staff' and 'other friends'); area of life; support behaviours; and interactional behaviours, and write in the totals at the end of bottom of the scoring sheet.

Totals on the scoring sheet may also be calculated and compared at different time points (e.g. every six or twelve months) to see if the social network of a particular individual has increased in size over time).

Exercise: Moving on

My Social Network

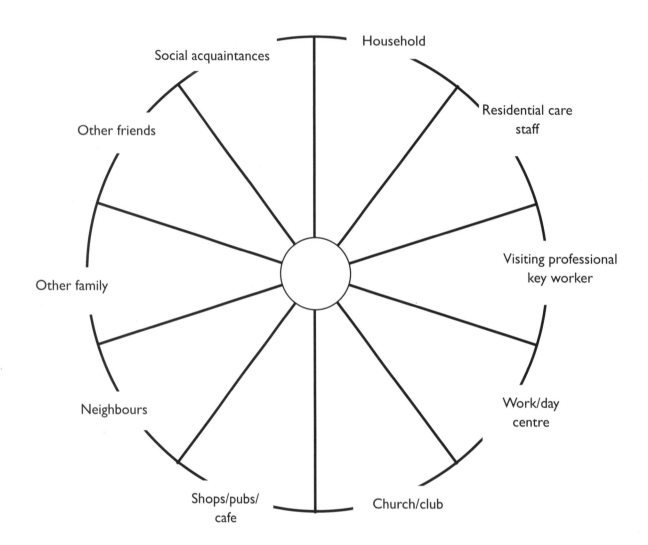

Display Sheet: Network Member (1)

1. Client/service user	2. Staff (paid carers)
3. Specialist/professional	4. Ex-staff
5. Volunteer/advocate	6. Service contact (pubs/cafes/shops)
7. Boy/girlfriend, spouse/partner	8. Other family (e.g. parents, siblings, children)
9. Social acquaintances (just people you know)	10. Other friends (without LD)
11. Employer, colleague, customer	

Area of Life

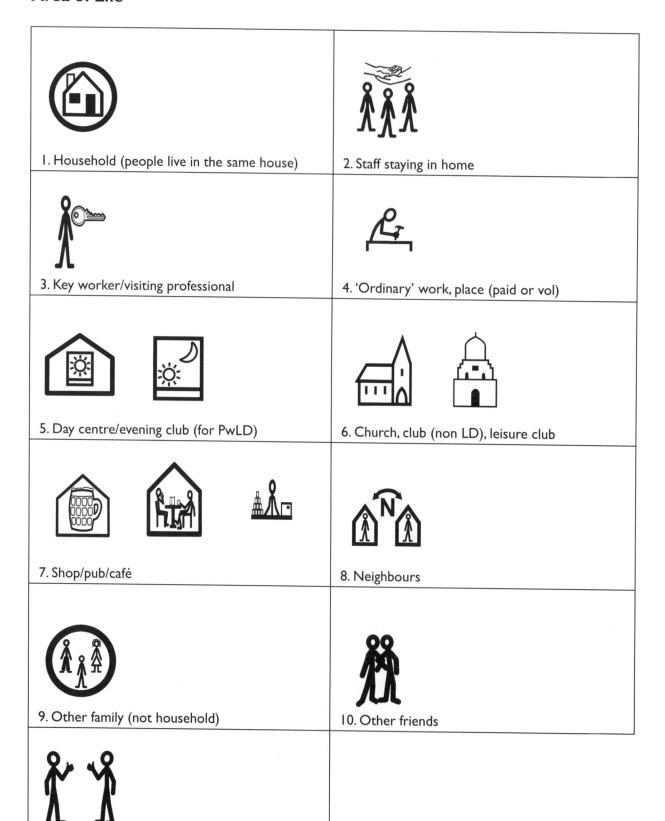

1. Household (people live in the same house)	2. Staff staying in home
3. Key worker/visiting professional	4. 'Ordinary' work, place (paid or vol)
5. Day centre/evening club (for PwLD)	6. Church, club (non LD), leisure club
7. Shop/pub/café	8. Neighbours
9. Other family (not household)	10. Other friends
11. Social acquaintances	

Display Sheet: Network Member (2)

Support behaviours: (☑ boxes)	Always/sometimes (1)	Hardly ever, never (2)
Personal (wash, dressing)		
Household (clean, cook, shop)		
Material (gives you money, cigs)		
Decisions		
Confide, you tell them your secrets		
Company (you like being together)		

Support behaviours: (☑ boxes)	Always/sometimes (1)	Hardly ever, never (2)
Invisible (keep an eye on you)		
Critical (nasty to you)		

Interactional behaviours:		
Reciprocity: (a) Do you help them and they help you? (b) Do you do things for each other?	Yes (1)	No (2)
Frequency: How often do you see this person?	Daily/weekly (1)	Monthly/less (2)
Duration: How long have you known this person?	Less than 5 years (1)	More than five years (2)
Relationship: Is this person your…	Best friend? (1)	You don't know very well? (2)

How do you feel about your relationship with this person?

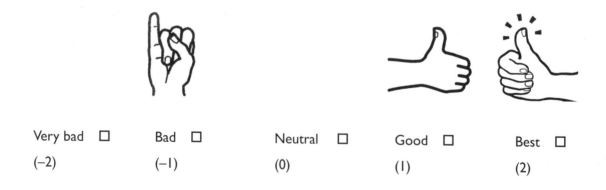

Very bad ☐   Bad ☐   Neutral ☐   Good ☐   Best ☐
(−2)   (−1)   (0)   (1)   (2)

Total scores of network contacts, the area of life they are derived from, and support provided by them																
Cn	Mem	AoL	Pers	House	Mat	D&F	Conf	Comp	Inv	Crit	Recip (a)	(b)	Freq	Dur	Rel	Feel

Key:

Cn	Contact
Mem	Member
AoL	Area of life
Pers	Personal support
House	Household support
Mat	Material support
D&F	Decision making and feedback
Conf	Confident
Comp	Companionship
Inv	Invisible support – 'Keep an eye on you'
Crit	Critical – 'nasty'
Recip	Reciprocity (a) – you help them and they help you Reciprocity (b) – you do things for each other
Freq	Frequency – 'daily, monthly, yearly contact'
Dur	Duration – 'how long known'
Rel	Relationship – 'best friend or someone not known well'
Feel	Feel about the relationship

Chapter 3

Loss of Home and Possessions

Mid pleasures and palaces though we may roam,
Be it ever so humble, there's no place like home…

J.H. Payne (1823)

Introduction

Losing things is a cumbersome and annoying yet common fact of life. Loss of a possession can be small and temporary (e.g. our reading glasses) or larger and permanent (e.g. our home). Whenever an external detail of our life changes we accept that we may lose certain things which may be replaced by new ones. For example, when we move location to take up a new job elsewhere, we experience loss of an old environment (e.g. moving from the country to a city). Generally we are able to rationalize what we lose (e.g. hills or sea, familiar people and places) with what we gain (e.g. new job and facilities, new opportunities to meet people and to do different things). People with learning disabilities and people with autism may experience the same losses and gains, but what is different about the experience for people with autism is that the element of choice is not always included in the loss–gain equation. Rather, they are often powerless to keep or lose things in their lives. For example, in Chapter 2 we discussed how people with learning disabilities and people with autism often find themselves experiencing multiple losses when a parent or family member dies. With an estimated 40 per cent of the population of people with learning disabilities living with their elderly parents, 10 per cent of whom live with a sole family carer over the age of 70 years (Walker and Walker cited in Blackman 2003), the experience of 'living out parents' is becoming more common. Parental death often results in the person with a learning disability including those with autism moving into residential care and consequently losing their sense of wellbeing and health through grief in addition to their previous home and social environment.

The impact of losing 'things' for people with autism

For people with autistic spectrum condition (ASC) losing an object means more than the annoyance of just being without it. Whenever an external detail changes, a person with ASC may experience a total change in their world.

The significance of objects

The nature of the difficulties of mono-attention, sensory sensitivities and information-processing means that many people on the autistic spectrum can be socially and communicatively isolated and extremely anxious. Because they do not experience the world in terms of human connections, they will often be 'object-focused' rather than 'people-focused'. This means that they may be very attached to specific objects or places, the loss of which will be far more traumatic than that experienced by a neuro-typical (NT).

Indeed for someone with autism who has a great memory for objective facts rather than subjective thoughts and feelings, losing an object can be very difficult. So for example, a person with ASC who is recounting an outing to watch their favourite football team play may not tell a story which includes what they 'liked' about the match or 'enjoyed' about the outing. Rather, they may mention sequentially the facts; where the match took place, what time, which train they took, which carriage they sat in, the time of the train, what they were wearing, the score and the colours of the football strip for both teams. The absence of their lost football strip/shirt will be difficult to bear.

For people with ASC, objects are often used as a comfort at times of stress or as a form of social support to enable them to do something they find difficult. The following case study of Jenny illustrates this point.

The case study of Jenny below enables us to see how in the face of adversity, objects replace support from other people. It does not leave much to the imagination to understand how devastating it would be for Jenny if she lost one of the gemstones.

Case study – Jenny

Jenny is in her twenties and is described as being on the autistic spectrum. She uses a number of polished gemstones to help her when she is anxious. They are objects that she has spent long periods of time staring at and so she knows every bit of them: the pattern of every line, every dimple, the texture, the smell, the weight of them in her hand. The stones have become so familiar to her that she no longer needs to process any information when she is looking at them. If she is anxious and feeling overwhelmed then she can focus on her stones to block everything else out and it enables her to 'bring her back to herself'. She states: 'In the middle of a meltdown I feel completely alone and really scared.' During these times, nothing in the 'people world' makes sense to her and nothing that people do can help her. However, her stones are the one object that offer her consistency and familiarity. They are the one thing that she is able to relate to and understand amid the confusion. If an object that offers such solace is taken away, intense loss is experienced.

Interpreting or sensing?

Donna Williams who was diagnosed with autism when she was 42 years old writes about the fact that people can process information in two distinct ways. These are namely 'interpreting' and 'sensing'. Explaining how she processes incoming information by 'sensing', Williams states:

> My brain seems to struggle to keep up with putting any concepts to words… Even when I do understand them [words], after three seconds the meaning of what I've heard is mostly jumbled and large chunks of it seem to have fallen away. I also often don't recognise objects when they are not in their expected place, and I can take up to two seconds to recognise the nature of an object. Unless it moves, unless I can experience it, it often doesn't mean anything at first. (Williams 2006, p.55)

The ability to understand language with meaning relies on absorbing the theme and feel of the communication as well as linking these with concepts and social uses. Whilst some people on the autistic spectrum are able to interpret incoming information by categorizing it and attaching meaning to the information, others like Donna process everything through 'sensing', that is, in terms of sequence, pattern, theme and feel. Clearly, someone who processes information through sensing rather than interpretation will struggle to form concepts and therefore will struggle to identify places and objects by way of recognizing their uses (Williams 2006).

Processing information simply by sensing will have a huge impact on an individual's understanding of losing a possession, even something as large as a house. For example, a NT who moves house will be able to ask for and understand explanations about why they are moving and where to. If a person has an ASC, as long as they are able to process information in an interpretive way, it is likely that they will understand at least basic explanations, especially if verbal explanations are accompanied with visual information such as pictures. They will also be able to understand the information surrounding the move by developing a concept of 'moving house' in their mind. They will be able to understand that they have physically left a house and that someone else is now living there.

However, this information is not accessible to people with an ASC if their primary way of processing information is by sensing. If they process information by simply absorbing the pattern, theme and feel of things, then they are not going to understand the process of moving home because their concept of 'home' is different. Their idea of 'home' was based on a mixture of smells, feelings, patterns and themes rather than a building made of bricks and mortar with a bedroom where they slept and a lounge where they watched TV. They may not even be aware that they have physically moved location. What they will be aware of is that nothing 'feels' the same whilst having no concept of where the familiar patterns, themes and feelings have gone. This means that when they move to a new house it may feel like 'the rooms are all in the wrong places, the furniture and windows and doors are not where they should be' (Williams 2006, p.282). This is something that we have all experienced to some degree. The following scenario may help you understand this process.

In your kitchen you keep the teabags in a cupboard above the kettle. At your friend's kitchen the teabags are kept in a cupboard on the opposite side of the room to the kettle. You know this because you have experienced it when you visited your friend's house previously. Yet every time you make a cup of tea in your friend's kitchen you open the cupboard above the kettle because this is the pattern you are used to. Nevertheless, you are able to process information in an interpretive way which enables you to problem solve by accessing your memory as to where your friend's teabags are kept. However, for someone who processes information only by sensing, once the pattern of the routine does not provide the expected outcome they are completely lost.

In the case of moving house, if the familiar patterns, feelings, smells, etc. are not replicated in the new home and the person with autism is unable to conceptualize where the old, familiar patterns, feelings and smells have gone, a deep sense of loss will be experienced. The person is likely to feel anxious, frightened and confused, and no verbal or visual explanations are going to make any sense.

Feeling disconnected

Owning possessions is related to control. Arguably the only things we can really control (as long as we have access to them) are tangible things, such as a book or item of clothing. Intangible things, such as beliefs or love, cannot be controlled. The way in which we control an object will be dictated by its size, situation, and whether it can be moved. Control of a particular space allows us to control the things within that space. Once we have obtained enough control of a thing to be in possession of it, that control can be relaxed without losing possession. Possession is lost if we lose something, someone takes it from us, or we throw it away. We may exhibit a range of emotions and behaviour when we lose something. For example, a lost/stolen wallet may result in expressions of frustration, anxiety and anger. A much-liked but lost football strip/shirt may result in disappointment and a little of our identity in addition since we associate ourselves with a particular football team. Such emotions and expressions may be heightened for people with autism since in general they have little control over space or things within space. If someone has very few possessions then the few they do have are more important to their identity (see Chapter 4). It is little wonder that people who resided in large institutions prior to their closure after the Community Care Act 1990 were described as being 'depersonalized' when most if not all of their possssessions were removed/stolen or lost during the course of their 'incarceration'.

The feeling of control associated with owning possessions such as a home is lost when the home and possessions are lost. Due to the importance of specific objects for many people on the spectrum and because of the way they may experience and conceptualize these objects, their loss can also result in a major loss of empowerment. Further, for some, the experience of loss of particular objects may result in an increased desire to isolate and disconnect from the world as a way of protecting themselves from the pain of such acute loss.

'Things' that can be lost

This section gives examples of both tangible and intangible things people with autism might have huge difficulties with losing.

Tangible possessions
KNOWN ENVIRONMENT

Familiar surroundings can be lost through moving to another location, house or room. Mitchell (2005) in his book *Glass Half Empty, Glass Half Full* recounts how at three years old moving house was very traumatic for him particularly when he thought that his toys packed in boxes and loaded into a removal van meant that they were being taken away for good. His routine had been disrupted and whilst he had felt settled and secure (if not altogether happy) in his previous community, moving house was perceived by him as very frightening.

During the moving period a person with ASC may be temporarily left without possessions, which reduces their sense of security in addition to losing things that amuse and occupy them. Moving to a new town might mean having to get to know different people with different dialects and sub-cultures. If the move includes a change in school, college or work then a change of classrooms and teachers or offices and colleagues can lead to confusion and a fear of getting lost. This might lead to mistakes which may make the person feel strange or stupid.

MEANINGFUL POSSESSIONS

The loss of a favourite toy or ornament would clearly be a serious loss to a person with autism. Less obvious is the importance that computers can have to someone with ASC.

Computers offer visual cues, repetition and sequencing, and do not make social demands on people who are using them (Lawson 2001). Rather computers can be used for educational and leisure purposes, and in particular for making social contact with other people without the requirements of social gestures such as smiling or listening to others' opinions. Further, computers do not offer distracting stimuli to invade an individual's concentration and interrupt thinking – unless of course the e-mail facility is switched on with a buzzer sounding every time an e-message arrives! A computer is predictable and controllable since its operation relies on clear-cut and structured rules. It will do whatever is asked of it (and not demand people to make verbal or non-verbal responses) so long as it is informed correctly of requests. It can provide great interest and excitement at a controlled pace (Lawson 2001). In short, it can be all things to all men/women to a greater or lesser extent depending on the wishes of the person using it. Given the versatility of using a computer and since people with ASC tend to be object-focused rather than people-focused, the loss of a computer can therefore be the most devastating thing in the world to them – even more traumatic than losing a person.

More abstract possessions
SAFETY

People protect themselves in a range of ways, by living in secure premises, insuring their property, checking out new friends and being careful in their sexual lives. However, people with autism find their sense of security in rules and rituals. If for example security has been compromised by a front door lock not working, a NT will experience a sense of unease about burglars until the lock is fixed. For a person with autism, it is the loss of the routine or ritual of unlocking the door in a particular way which may upset their sense of security most. Such a sudden variation in an external detail can constitute a total change in their world around them and may lead to extreme levels of anxiety.

FAMILIAR ROUTES

Changes in routes to particular places – for example when road-works prevent taking the same route to college, work or the local day centre – will again constitute a change in routine and may lead to confusion, fear and anxiety and other behavioural responses including rocking or crying.

SEASONAL CHANGES

Changes in weather and temperature usually mean we swap our clothes, shoes and activities for more appropriate ones (e.g. we sunbathe during the summer when the sun shines, but in the winter we put on more clothes) (Lawson 2001). However, someone on the autistic spectrum observes that the sun also shines during the winter and so to have to change or put on more clothes does not appear to make any sense. Someone with autism therefore might wear shorts and a t-shirt on a cold but sunny winter's day. If challenged about the appropriateness of an item of clothing and asked to change (e.g. asked to put on trousers instead of shorts), the person with autism may find having to change their attire very difficult. Such a change might have a negative effect on the individual causing them to go through some of the emotions associated with grief.

ACHIEVEMENT AND SUCCESS

Whilst siblings of people with autism can feel a mixture of feelings such as protectiveness, embarrassment, resentfulness and guilt (Frender and Schiffmiller 2007), people with autism can feel and experience jealousy and envy of their NT siblings.

Sometimes other people put unrealistic expectations on people with autism (concerning their abilities) based on socially constructed and media-based myths (for example, the film *Rain Man*, in which a man with an ASC could calculate complicated mathematical problems). When a person with autism does not exhibit such gifts and talents there is a sense of disappointment from family and friends. This disappointment can be transferred to the person with autism who may then feel frustrated and sad. They may also feel that the things they want or aspire to in life are simply not possible or the opportunity to grasp them has been lost due to society's disabling response to their difficulties. For example, Grant and Ramcharan (2005) discussed how a woman called Jo dreamt about having her own home in the city 'near to the action'. However, she did not want to share this dream with members of staff for fear of losing her present accommodation. This led Grant and Ramcharan to conclude that sometimes expectations of individuals (e.g. owning a home) are at odds with staff which can stifle any further aspirations a service user might have.

Loss of home and possessions

Computer

Stone

Stick

Clock

If you have an ASC you may use objects to comfort you during stressful situations,

or as a form of social support to enable you to do something

you find difficult.

If an object that offers this kind of support is no longer available,

you may feel the loss.

For example, the feeling of being in control associated with owning

possessions such as a home, is lost when the home and possessions are lost.

Some people have specific objects which they experience and

understand in a unique way.

Losing these objects can also result in a major loss of empowerment.

If you lose an important object you may want to be alone, away from the world.

This seems to help protect you from the pain of such an acute loss.

The ability to understand language with meaning relies on taking in the theme and feel of the communication as well as linking these with concepts and social uses.

If you have autism, you may be able to interpret incoming

information by putting it into categories and attaching meaning to those categories

(e.g. when someone asks 'Can you make a sandwich' you categorize the sentence into 'Can you' 'make' and 'sandwich'). You might therefore reply 'Yes' because you know that you *can* (are able to) make a sandwich but you don't actually set about making it because you are not presently in the

kitchen where you always make sandwiches and you cannot see

any bread or butter to make the sandwich.

Or, you might process information through 'sensing'.

You understand something in terms of sequence, pattern, theme and feel.

For example, when someone tells you 'Let's have some dinner' at 2 o'clock in the afternoon, you understand it is 'OK to eat some dinner' only because you have just finished a task which is always followed by having food,

or you can smell food. Without these sensing cues, you might think it strange to have some food at that time of day.

If the familiar patterns, feelings, smells, etc. are not replicated in a new situation or object, and you are unable to understand where the old, familiar patterns, feelings and smells have gone, you may experience a deep sense of loss.

You may feel anxious, frightened and confused and no verbal or visual explanations are going to make any sense. You will need help to understand what has happened.

Worksheet 3.1

Identifying the individual's information-processing style

Carers can often miss the significance that a loss of a possession (or home) holds for a person with an ASC. The first indication that a person with an ASC is experiencing the emotions of loss can be an increase in behaviour including aggression, withdrawal or obsessive/ritualistic behaviour. It is therefore important to take time to identify correctly what has been lost and attempt to understand what significance the object held for the individual. To understand the importance of the object we need to know how the individual experienced it. The first step is to discover the person's primary way of processing information.

Aim: to find out whether the primary way of processing information is interpretive or sensing.

Objective: once established, to be able to decide how best to help the person come to terms with and move on from the loss.

Exercise: Identifying the individual's information-processing style

Use the following guidance, ticking and adding up the boxes to help you discover the person's primary way of processing information.

Interpretive	✓	Sensing	✓
Learns best using instructions (verbal, written or visual).		Learns best by pattern and routine (i.e. by repeatedly doing).	
Understands when given verbal, written or visual explanations.		Is unable to understand or learn from explanations. Learns only from the consequences of actions when repeated over and over.	
Relies on stored learning for emotional expression. May have trouble linking the way their body feels with their communication and behaviour. For example, may say 'I am upset' without sounding cross, or may laugh when angry.		Uses the movement and sound of their body to express emotion. May rock their body when feeling sad or make high-pitched squeals when excited.	
Enjoys stimulation through language (i.e. will seek people out to talk to them).		May spend hours lost in a pattern (i.e. repeatedly making the same movement or staring at the same object).	
Very literal in their understanding of language (e.g. interpreting the saying 'I have butterflies in my tummy' to mean that the person really does have butterflies in their tummy).		May use smell, touch or sound to test familiarity (i.e. rather than using vision they may smell or touch objects or people to recognize them).	
May fixate on ideas that they see as logical but which are very narrow (e.g. may have heard that drinking water is healthy and want to drink water all day).		May use objects in a sensory way rather than the purpose they were designed for (e.g. spinning placemats, flicking rubber gloves, flapping books/magazines).	
Total		**Total**	

Worksheet 3.2

Demonstrating a particular loss

Aim: to talk about or/and demonstrate a particular loss

Objective: to understand about the loss of something like a home or possessions and to understand that all people experience loss in different ways

Option 1: for people whose information processing is primarily interpretive

For this activity you will need an open attitude and a motivation to ask others for help, plus a willingness to spend time searching for all kinds of aids to use.

Option 2: for people whose information processing is primarily sensing

Below are some suggestions that may help

1. Remember that verbal, written or other visual explanations are not going to help the person understand the change/loss so do not complicate the situation by trying to use these methods.

2. If possible, get a comprehensive picture of how the old house was laid out and replicate this as far as possible in the new home

3. Make sure you are aware of the day to day routines that the person had and again try to replicate these. Where these routines need to change try to change tiny bits at a time giving the person a chance to become familiar with the new patterns in their life.

4. Use intensive interaction to help reach the individual and to begin communicating in a way that they are familiar with.[1]

5. Where an object has been lost, support the person to find a replacement. Try to identify the characteristics of the item that the person related to giving the person access to other objects that share the same characteristics.

6. Never underestimate the importance an object holds for an individual or the acute loss they may feel when it has gone.

---

[1] For more information on this technique, read Hewett, D. and Nind, M. (eds) (1998) *Interaction in Action: Reflections on the Use of Intensive Interaction.* London: David Fulton Publishers; or watch the Intensive Interaction Video by Caldwell (2002) *Learning the Language: A Video-based Resource on Building Relationships with People with Severe Learning Disabilities.* Brighton: Pavilion.

Exercise: Demonstrating a particular loss

Remember that quite a few individuals with autism do not like being touched unless they initiate it.

1. Draw a picture of home or lost possession from memory or cut out and stick a photo or picture from a magazine in the box below.

2. Draw yourself next to the home

    -   Point to the drawing
    -   Take the drawing of the house away
    -   Draw a picture or plan of the building which replaces the old house
    -   Name the function of each room. Was the house big? How many bedrooms? What did you do in each room?

3. Next discuss the following:

- What has changed? Stick labels on the home. Where have the things gone?

- Draw how you felt when the change occurred. Were you angry? Sad? Disappointed? Use the following symbols:

  Angry   Sad   Upset   Happy

4. Make a collage on a separate sheet of paper about 'how I felt' when the change happened. Use books and illustrations about homes from the local library or cut out from magazines to do this.

- Place the work in a ring binder. You can return to this file and look at various items to remember the changes that have occured.

Worksheet 3.3
Role playing

Aim: to help the person to act out in clear steps what occurred.

Objective: to enable the person to work through the loss in their minds.

Exercise: Role playing

Help the person to act out in clear steps what occurred. For example:

Loss of Home

    (a)   Have the person pretend to be sitting in their old home.

    (b)   Then have them play the role of the person telling them about the move.

    (c)   Have them act out their feelings, what they said.

    (d)   Have them act out what new things they do, where things are in the new home.

After this, it is sometimes helpful to physically take them back to the old house to literally show them that new people are living in it.

Loss of Computer

    (a)   Have the person pretend to be sat working on their computer.

    (b)   Have them act out what they did when it stopped working.

    (c)   Then have them play the role of the person telling them that it needed to go to the shop to get fixed/that it could not be fixed.

    (d)   Have them act out their feelings, what they said.

    (e)   Have them act out how they will feel when it is fixed/they get a new one.

For someone with a high IQ (someone with Asperger's Syndrome) it may be useful simply to listen to their description of what has gone wrong with the computer. We provide the example of Chris, who recently talked to us about the hardware failure on his computer. The following monologue illustrates the need to patiently listen to what may seem like endless sentences.

> 'The hard drive has been corrupted and my data lost. I have tried to re-partition the hard drive myself and that can't be done as the hard drive has been physically damaged and it needs to be replaced. I need to take the computer down to the shop in town and buy a new hard drive from them with an operating system and I can leave the computer with them and they will put it into my computer and then I will come back the following day and the computer will be fixed and I will be able to use it again. If it is a software failure it might only be necessary to install the operating system and I might not need to buy a hard drive.
>
> I had my work saved on my computer and it feels awful and it is annoying and inconvenient. I have replayed the situation, and I have been dwelling on it, I imagined what I could have done, what I should have done differently. I'd like to talk about it with a person about how it might have happened, how it can be fixed and prevent it happening in the future. I want to talk about it to a person who understands computers. In my case I find that will only apply when talking to someone who understands about the nature of the problem.'

N.B. Because people on the autistic spectrum can struggle to comprehend the concept of time, it can help to provide a visual representation of how many days it will be before the person gets the computer back/gets a new one.

Chapter 4

Loss of Role and Identity

All my life people have thought I was odd. I don't want them to know about my condition... I'm a student and that's it.

Abraham Barts – a person with autism

Introduction

Why is it important to have a role in life?

How we socially interact (what we do, what we say and talk about) with others is very much tied up with the roles we have and the roles we play within our families (e.g. mother, father, carer, sibling, cousin) as well as within wider society (e.g. employee, employer, swimmer, dancer, etc.). Certain occupational roles have a higher status than others (e.g. doctor vs bus driver) and roles include a number of norms which define how a person occupying that role is supposed to behave/act. For example, the role of 'care worker' includes expectations of behaving in a 'caring', 'supportive' and 'sensitive' way. The role of 'teacher' includes providing information and instruction. Social roles are usually defined by society but can be unclear or vague. Nevertheless, they tend to regulate and organize our behaviour. Some people have a variety of roles (e.g. part-time teacher and part-time carer to elderly parent). Others talk in terms of having one role (e.g. key worker).

We learn about particular roles and the normative behaviours which go with them during childhood 'role playing', for example by taking on the roles and sometimes costumes/uniforms of 'Doctors and Nurses' or 'Cowboys and Indians' and via team game-playing; for example, we learn the role of goal attack (or striker) in relation to goal keeper in a game of netball (or football). This is what Mead (1934) called 'role-taking'. Mead argued that we develop our own self-concepts by placing ourselves in the position or role of the person we are interacting with. By doing this we can interpret how our behaviours might affect theirs, understand why they respond to our behaviour in a particular way, and act accordingly. For example, if we say or do something which clearly angers another person, we might modify our behaviour in the future. By being self-conscious we can consider the consequences of our actions, have some idea of how others view us and know what is expected of us in our roles. It is these roles which help to define our personal and social identities. However, someone with autism who is mono-tracked will find it difficult to see themselves as players within social situations, which they will experience as isolated pictures. They will therefore find it hard to see their own role or self-concept.

Identity

Identity may be defined as the construction of one's own sense of self. We develop our own identities through the social situations in which we find ourselves and through the way in which our social interactions with others relate to our self-concept (including self-esteem, self-image and self-evaluation). We also define ourselves in comparison to others (Mishler 1999). By having a sense of ourselves we can understand our place in and our actions on social situations (Vermeulen 2000).

Throughout a lifetime our roles might multiply, change or diminish (e.g. on retirement we cease to have the role of 'employee'). Likewise our identities are not fixed but shift according to the roles we play out at any one time. Similarly, the obligations and social status attached to these roles also change. Goffman (1959, 1962b) argued that we can present ourselves and act in particular ways during social occasions (for example, trying to impress others or 'save face') in order to create or win the most socially desired identity available to us (Alexander and Wiley 1981). As society increasingly adopts an illusory world of perfection (e.g. perfect body, eyesight, possessions, job), so we are defined according to these markers. Such a society tends to appraise an individual by the way they behave, talk and look.

Although a person with autism may have no distinguishing physical features, they may be viewed by other people as different or 'imperfect' because of their unusual social behaviour and conversation skills (Bloom 2005). They may learn by rote certain norms and rules for specific situations only to find these are not appropriate or acceptable in other social contexts (e.g. hugging complete strangers). Unable to learn from their experiences, they will make the same social mistakes time after time, and get labelled by others as eccentric, odd or strange, and possibly be expelled from the social group. Writing about learning disabilities, Todd and Blackman (2005) recount how Sudnow's (1967) idea of 'social death' still remains a reality for some people who are socially excluded from mainstream society. Ward (2001) goes so far as to debate whether a new eugenics movement has crept into our society, where disability is seen as something to be prevented, as illustrated by the fact that the amniocentesis is available to detect imperfect foetuses.

Sexual identity

Finally, sexuality is core to self-identity (Foucault 1990). Issues including sexual behaviour, representations of gender, knowledge of risks, contraception, parenting and the formation and maintenance of relationships are all integral to our identity which includes how we present ourselves in the community. For many people with autism, emotional and physical intimacy are major factors missing from their lives altogether or are carried out as covert activities. All around them they see people in intimate relationship roles: parents, adult siblings and staff, reinforced daily by images in newspapers and on the television. Historically the sexuality of people with disabilities has been both denied and feared (Craft and Craft 1979; McCarthy 1999). Very often, people with autism will be thought of and treated as 'eternal children' (Kempton 1972) and their sexuality dismissed.

In fact, people with autism have the same emotional and sexual drives as other people. However, they tend to be given less information (Gordon 1972) or are actively prevented from getting into intimate relationships which are seen as potentially dangerous (McCarthy 1999) or difficult to manage. Until recently routine sterilization of women with learning disabilities including people with autism occurred in many services. This reflects the view still held by many, that people with disabilities are unable to control themselves. People with autism may find intimate relationships difficult to bear (see Chapter 2), but this does not mean to say they do not want them and do not need support to engage in them. The role of being 'a partner', whether it is a sexual relationship or not, is an important part of an individual's identity. The appropriate options for developing this part of a person's identity should be explored via person-centred planning.

How identities are diminished, devalued and damaged

Within an interactionist perspective, labelling theory states that the way in which society reacts to and labels an individual's behaviour alters their social identity (Lemert 1951). Goffman (1962) showed how formal labelling (e.g. arrest or imprisonment) and informal labelling (e.g. stigmatization of people with disabilities, including mental health problems) led to diminished self-concepts and devalued social and personal identities and roles. In the 1960s, Northern European countries developed the philosophy of 'normalization' as a means through which services might 'create an existence for the mentally retarded as close to normal living conditions as possible' (Bank-Mikkelson 1980, p.56). It was adopted and adapted in North America to a philosophy of 'social role valorization', where Wolfensberger (1983) stressed the need for people at risk of devaluation to be supported to gain or be given social roles which are valued by society. In their manual for evaluating services, Wolfensberger and Glen (1975) argued that services should help all adults with learning disabilities to attain a culturally valued analogue (CVA) found in, for example, fully paid employment. However, as Ramcharan *et al.* (1997) argued, such a social role valorization model was inherently stigmatizing for people who were unable to access paid employment. Similarly, Szivos and Griffiths (1990) critiqued social role valorization, stating it emphasized image and competency as well as assimilation into mainstream values. This they say encourages passing as 'normal' whatever that may be. They argued instead for 'consciousness raising', with individuals gaining support from a positive group identity.

In an attempt to rid ourselves of stigmatized labels, we may engage in 'resistance to labelling' (Prus 1975) by taking on other, more acceptable roles. On the other hand, if the label is useful, or if relationships with others are dependent on it (Stryker 1968), or there appears to be little chance of shaking it off, we might engage in behaviour which fulfils the prophecy. In the stark reality of a society which values perfection, and whilst we wait for educational awareness programmes which teach positive perspectives of disability to have an impact on subsequent generations, it is important for people with disabilities to have access to acquiring socially valued roles within society. O'Brien (1987) interprets this need in terms of five fundamental accomplishments for service delivery for individuals with learning disabilities which are also relevant for people with autism. These are: competence (e.g. opportunities to learn new skills); presence (e.g. being included in community facili-ties); community participation (e.g. opportunity to engage in meaningful activities including paid employment); choice (e.g. options of going to the local pub and drinking with friends); and respect (e.g. support to self-present positively and be perceived by carers in a positive light).

When stereotypes, labels and stigma begin – social identities are lost

Our society celebrates diversity yet continues to devalue the lives of people who are different, including people with autism. Social responses to 'differentness' can be harsh. Whilst in the nineteenth century people with undiagnosed autism were kept behind closed doors out of sight of mainstream society (read the story of 'Wooden Tony' by Lucy Lane Clifford (1882), which Charlotte Moor (1982a) describes as a 'rather beautifiul descrip-tion of autism'; for a biography of Clifford, see Chisholm 2002), despite new advances in diagnosis, people with autism continue to be faced with stigmatized, discriminatory and hurtful attitudes from other members of the community such as health professionals, employers and neighbours. Myths and stereotypes about people with autism (e.g. that they cannot make eye contact, smile, show affection, engage in reciprocal play or think in the abstract, or that they are 'difficult', 'challenging' or 'strange') also continue to abound, which highlights the lack of understanding people have of the condition. Whitman (2004) argues that pejorative attitudes to people with autism also stem from a time of institutional-ized treatment before the development of early intervention programmes. These views also do not take into account individual differences. In fact people with autism can demonstrate amazing development over time. Nevertheless, such societal attitudes can act as a strong barrier to social inclusion, especially if they remain unchallenged (McConkey 2005). We can recount many conversations with carers and families of people with autism as well as people who have autism who have experienced name calling, people talking behind their backs, being bossed around, or patronized. This is because although autism is being diagnosed more regularly, many people know little about it and so their images and beliefs about autism are stereotyped, negative and mistaken. Moore (2002a, 2003) recounts how her two sons do not appear to be ambitious and are indifferent to the opinion of teachers or pupils. She further suggests that similar behaviour in other children with autism has led to inclusion in mainstream schools as being disastrous even though their IQ is high. Such children, she argues, have not and are not being catered for by societal institutions, but it is the children who are labelled as failures, and they in turn have been traumatized by the failure. Thus, a lack of understanding of what autism entails can lead to prejudiced behaviour by teachers and colleagues including labelling and can ultimately lead to some people with autism having a poor self-concept leading to a lost or damaged personal and social identity.

It is against this backdrop of labels that people with autism and their families have to live and negotiate relationships, whilst at the same time suffering from the threat of, or actual, rejection and isolation. Rejection is a form of loss which can make people feel and believe they are unloved and unlovable. In Figure 4.1 we show how the process of rejection is interlinked with devalued roles.

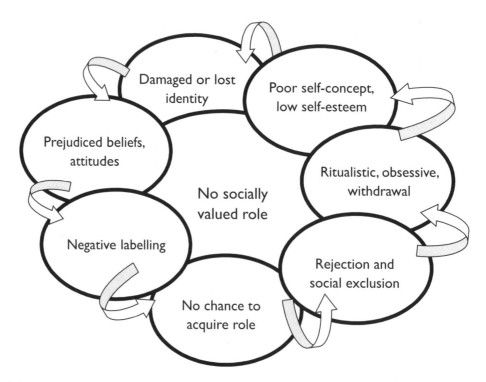

Figure 4.1 The link between role and damaged or lost identities

Courtesy stigma

Many parents who have children with autism will suffer the loss and experience the grief (at various levels and degrees) of having a child who is 'different' from the majority of other children, even though they may not look different. Each family member may grieve at different rates, different times and different stages (see Chapter 1, Figure 1.2 for stages of grief) and this can add strain to an already traumatized family (Bicknell 1983). This is often compounded by changes in their own social networks of relationships. Whilst some families feel that their child's autism has resulted in otherwise untapped generosity from professionals, friends and family (Whitman 2004), as demands on family time increase, socialization with friends and extended family may diminish (Donenberg and Baker 1993). Further, particular friends or extended kin may have difficulties in adapting to and dealing with autism, leading to avoidance, isolation and ultimately a lack of social support. Whitman (2004) describes how parents of children with autism go through excruciating social embarrassment caused by the unkind comments from neighbours, other parents and social acquaintances who give out a message that it is a tragedy or personal burden to have a child with autism. In effect, parents suffer from *courtesy stigma*, that is, they share the stigma of the stigmatized by association with them. This is particularly acute if the behaviour of a child has not been diagnosed properly or at all. Some may engage in a 'cover up' of the true status of their child's impairment by denying there is anything different about them or making wild claims about their intelligence. This is similar to large-scale studies which have shown that family members believe their relationship with a person with mental illness should be kept hidden or otherwise be a source of shame (Angermeyer, Schulze and Dietrich 2003; Phillips *et al.* 2002). Siblings have also been shown to experience embarrassment as they introduce their brother/sister with autism to their friends (Roeyers and Mycke 1995). Whilst it could be argued that there is a danger of the effects of courtesy stigma (such as guilt or shame) carried by family members being transferred to the child, Goffman (1962b) also argued that people with shared stigma can at least provide each other with a 'circle of lament' to which they can withdraw for moral support.

Being part of a group with a negative social identity

Some people on the autistic spectrum will find being part of an 'autism group' or group of service users shameful. This can lead them to display discriminatory behaviour, such as social avoidance of fellow stigmatized members. People with autism may not wish to speak to fellow service users when they bump into each other at public places. The label 'autism' or 'service user' may also deny opportunities to carry out ordinary adult social roles, since being a service user can lead to the adults with autism being trapped within childish roles. Thus they carry the burden of the stigmatized 'service user' label with its connotations of dependence and lack of autonomy. When people with autism do find an opportunity to move away from a stigmatized group, and are able to define themselves as members of the majority, they may stigmatize their previous group as a membership mechanism.

A few people with autism have managed to carve out political roles for themselves, encouraged by the advocacy and self-advocacy movements. In 2003 The National Autistic Society published a brief report entitled *Autism: The Demand for Advocacy*. The report highlighted difficulties advocacy organizations have in working with individuals with autism. These include (NAS 2003a, p.2):

- lack of understanding of ASC
- communication difficulties
- difficulties people with autism have when they are faced with 'choice'
- difficulties in finding out what the individual wants
- problems in building relationships with the individual
- gaining informed consent
- ethics of advocating for people with communication difficulties.

In the same year the NAS report *Autism: Rights in Reality* highlighted that only 11 per cent of carers in the UK stated that the adult they cared for had ever used an independent advocate (NAS 2003b). People with autistic spectrum condition (ASC) are beginning to provide first-hand insights into the challenges of living with this complex disability. Like other disability groups they are becoming more organized, and a small section of the autism population is starting to speak out about their lives and their rights. Many individuals with autism are providing their expertise to organizations and being invited to speak at conferences. This sharing of knowledge will hopefully have a profound effect on the future attitude of society and the value they place on people with autism. However, for the most part, the ideal of a valued group identity as charted by Szivos and Griffiths (1990) has yet to become a reality for many people with autism.

How having a socially valued role helps our personal and social identity

Goffman (1962) argued that the self-isolate who lacks daily social intercourse with others can become depressed, anxious and suspicious. However, having a role other than 'service user' provides an excuse for social interaction, as well as self-esteem. In particular, having responsibility for another person which incorporates giving support rather than always receiving it has been reported as important to individuals' own personal identity. For example, Julie who has autism has recently started going out with James who is a neuro-typical (NT). She says: 'It is nice to go out with him; I help him and he helps me...in lots of ways.' Clearly, Julie has grown in confidence and self-esteem. Part of her personal identity for the time being is wrapped around her role as 'girlfriend'. Similarly, this role also enables her to move towards a more socially acceptable identity. Similar findings of a study amongst people with mental health difficulties were found by Forrester-Jones and Barnes (in press). They argued that individuals can control information they give to others much more effectively if they are acting out roles which they can describe and discuss. So, Julie needs only to talk about her role as girlfriend if she wants to, and is able to manage the 'stigma' of 'being autistic' in a way which is functional to her own identity. Julie's role and self-concept is therefore above and beyond that of 'service user'. At the same time, the social identity of autism can enable people with autism who support others to do this on a flexible basis only, on the understanding that the commitment can be broken on individuals' own terms, according to how fit-for-role they feel. This dual identity – what Goffman (1962, p.159) called 'stigmatized and normal complementary roles' – can usefully coexist.

Problems arise when roles are lost. For example, relationships sometimes break up and periods of employment end. Apart from the tangible losses, such as social network members, social support, finance and structure to the day, loss of role will affect a person's self-esteem, self-worth and ultimately how they view themselves, their personal and social identity. The following case study of Zac illustrates this point.

The case study below provides a warning against making life-changing decisions during the first year of bereavement (Parkes 1970). It also shows the importance of roles and how their loss can result in a kind of secondary bereavement (Blackman 2003). Walker, Walker and Ryan (1996) argue that the lives of people with disabilities are seen

---

Case study – Zac

Zac had what can be described as an inter-dependent relationship with his elderly mum. Whilst she had cared for Zac alone for many years after his dad died, Zac did the shopping, some cleaning and would make a sandwich for his mum each evening. Zac's role in the house was largely invisible to staff. When Zac's mum died, he was moved to a supported living environment where staff did most household chores. Although Zac and staff went shopping to the local supermarket once a week, it was not the same as the more frequent local shopping he had been used to. Zac did not like the large supermarket, and staff complained that he would suddenly 'throw a tantrum' whenever they tried to take him. Eventually, his key worker set out to do some person-centred planning with Zac and found out about his former 'role'. Once his behaviour in the supermarket could be explained, staff were able to adapt house routines, and Zac now visits the nearest local SPAR shop every few days.

---

generally as purpose-less or role-less due to the limited expectations people without disabilities have of them. This raises important issues about how individuals can be supported to regain or find substitute roles, engaging in healthy risk-taking activities as they attempt to rebuild their lives. Space to negotiate identities of choice rather than negative 'sticky' ones should be at the heart of support. Within person-centred planning for example, providing support to engage in meaningful paid or unpaid activities which lead to opportunities for developing relationships can help restore damaged identities. In the absence of socially validated roles, which paid work for example provides, individuals need the chance to give and receive social support which is crucial in helping them develop an acceptable and valued sense of self. Person-centred planning should also incorporate guidance to informal carers and families about how best to harness social support so that their clients can lead meaningful lives with valued roles through a sense of reciprocity and social belonging.

How autism can affect personal identity

As suggested above, to develop a sense of identity you need to have a simultaneous sense of self and other. Without this it is difficult to understand what self is and where it ends. One of the difficulties with being mono-attentive is that you may have a tendency to swing between a state of 'all self' (where you are not even aware of other people's existence let alone your impact on them) to a state of 'all other' where you are very aware of other people but unable to access your own feelings. Donna Williams describes this as 'feeling as if you have disappeared' (Williams 2006, p.298).

If you don't use or understand language, you are unlikely to think in words. You may think in pictures or you may think in sensations. Again this has an impact on the way in which you gain a perception of self and other. If you process information mainly by sensing, then you do not hold concepts in your head in any conscious way. This means that how you develop your sense of identity will be very different from that of NTs. If you tend to grasp concepts only through direct sensory experience, then you 'sense' the world rather than conceive it. Concepts are difficult to hold on to because once the sensory stimulation stops, the concept floats away. This is similar to most babies who are too busy being consciously engaged in thought processes. Most typically developing children have formed an ability to conceive the world rather than simply sense it by the age of three. Hence they begin to grasp a sense of their own identity. This process can happen much later for people on the autistic spectrum and may not happen until adulthood in some cases (e.g. Williams 2006).

Finally, it must be remembered that some people on the autistic spectrum may have disconnected from their bodies as a coping mechanism. For many of us our body is a part of who we are and how we express ourselves. However, if you have been physically abused or have had long periods of ill health, there is a tendency to disconnect from the body so that it is no longer part of 'self'. Likewise, if you are living in an institutional environment where you are often forced to do things against your will or to someone else's timetable, you do not feel in control of your body. One way of coping is to disassociate from your body so that it becomes a part of the outside world rather than a part of you (Williams 2006). Once again this means that how you experience a sense of identity will be very different from how others experience it.

For people on the autistic spectrum, identity issues can cause depression, isolation and depersonalization. In some cases such issues underpin the development of anxiety disorders, and they can aggravate compulsive disorders.

Fact Sheet 4.1

Loss of role and identity

If you have an ASC you may see-saw between a state of

'all self' (where you are not even aware of other people's existence let alone your impact on them) and a state of

'all other' (where you are very aware of other people but unable to access your own feelings).

If you tend to grasp concepts only through direct sensory experience then you 'sense' the world rather than conceive it. Concepts are difficult to hold on to because once the sensory stimulation stops the concept floats away.

Therefore, how you develop your sense of identity will be very different from that of neuro-typical people.

Identity is about the people you interact with (the people you talk to and do things with)

And how they make you feel –   good   or   bad?

A man called Erving Goffman said in 1962[1] that if people lack

daily social intercourse with others, they can become

depressed,   anxious   and suspicious.

However, having a role other than 'service user' provides an

---

1   Goffman, E. (1962a) *Asylums*. New York: Anchor.

excuse for social interaction, as well as self-esteem.

In particular, having responsibility for another person, which includes helping them rather than them always helping you, is very important to your own personal identity.

Identity issues can cause depression, isolation and

depersonalization.

In some cases such issues are the cause of anxiety disorders

and they can aggravate compulsive disorders.

Mini person-centred plan – Who am I?

Before working on the loss of role, it is important to establish who the person perceives themselves to be, and gain a fuller sense of the person's identity.

Aim: to describe aspects about the person, to map the person's life in terms of social network, interests, future aspirations.

Objective: to establish who the person is, to support the person to rediscover who they are behind the problems they have.

My Social Network

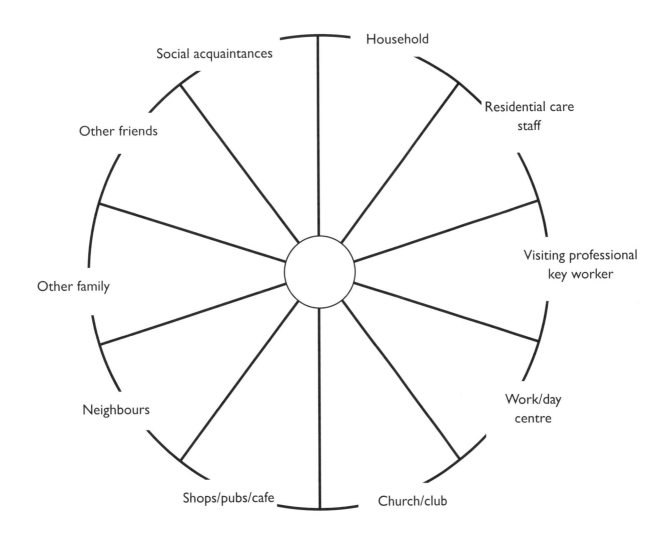

Exercise: Mini person-centred plan –Who am I?

1. Identify who is in the person's circle of support by completing a **My Social Network** circle (see also Worksheet 2.3).

2. With input from the person themselves and those in their circle of support, put together a **life map and memory box**. This can be done in a variety of different ways depending on the person's communication abilities and sensory preferences. It can be done as a photo album, a box of items that hold particular memories or even a variety of bottles with particular smells that are associated with specific memories.

3. You only really get to know a person by doing things with them. **Activity taster sessions** are a way of trying activities and identifying what a person really likes. For example you might know that a person likes music but you are not sure what type of music and due to their limited communication skills they are unable to tell you. You could do a series of taster sessions to identify the person's preferences.

For example:

*   Play three different types of music (rock, pop, country). Whilst each one is playing, record in a factual way what the person does (e.g. walks out of the room, dances, indicates that they want more, etc.).

*   Repeat this process a couple of times, playing the types of music in a different order each time and record what the person does.

*   A similar process can be used for a variety of activities and is particularly useful for people who do not use verbal communication.

4. Now think about the following questions and discuss with your participant (you can use sections of Worksheet 1.1 in Chapter 1).

    *   How do you describe yourself?

    *   How do others see you?

    *   Are you expected to be 'someone' or 'something'? (e.g. are you expected to be unable to do things for yourself?)

    *   What things in your life make you feel good about yourself?

    *   Do you have any unrealistic self-expectations?

    *   Are you trying to please anyone?

    *   Do you aspire to being like anyone? (e.g. Princess Diana, David Beckham)

Are there ways in which any issues which have become apparent in answering the above questions can be alleviated?

Worksheet 4.2

Loss of a role

Aim: to structure a discussion about a previous role the person had, what it entailed and the importance of it to them.

Objective: to acknowledge that the role was important for them and to help them see that it has now gone.

Exercise: Loss of a role

Using a whiteboard (or electronic equivalent) or paper and pen, draw a series of circles side by side. In the first circle, write (or draw or paste pictures to show) something that denotes the role the person with ASC had, and the behaviours that went with the role, as well as the good things about the role and how it made the person feel. Since it is likely that the person will have more than one role, repeat this with one circle for each role (see the example below).

For example, Alan, who recently lost his job packing boxes with sweets and crisps for a small supported employment company providing tuck shop provisions to local businesses.

Role: brother
What I did: helped my younger sister
Why was it good? I like my sister
How it made me feel? good

Role: worker
What I did: packed chocolate and crisps into a box
Why was it good? I got paid
How it made me feel? good, I can buy things

Role: friend
What I did: chatted to them on the computer
Why was it good? I like having friends
How it made me feel? good

Worksheet 4.3

What happened? – Sharing feelings

Aim: to demonstrate how one of the roles you had has now been lost. We will do this by deleting or wiping out the picture of the role. We will talk about how you felt when you lost this particular role (the role of worker, son/daughter). We will also talk about when people call you names or when people are not nice to you because you have autism (stigma and rejection).

Objective: to talk about what it means to lose a role and to acknowledge that this role has now gone.

Exercise: What happened? – Sharing feelings

N.B. When any relationship ends, there are often mixed emotions. If a person has learned to suppress certain emotions by being taught to 'be strong' and 'don't cry' they may try to suppress their feelings. But feelings do not go away – they seek release either through behaviour or physical symptoms. Be specific and talk through the feelings the person has.

Using a whiteboard (or electronic equivalent) or paper and pen:

1.   Use the same circles drawn in the previous exercise (Worksheet 4.2).

2.   Wipe out or delete the role which has now been lost.

3.   Discuss why the job/role has gone. What happened?

4.   Draw in feelings (these may include sad faces).

5.   Discuss how other people react to you (stigma).

6.   Note, whilst the previous role which is now wiped out is lost, the other roles still remain.

For example, Alan still has two roles left:

Role: brother
What I did: helped my younger sister
Why was it good? I like my sister
How it made me feel? good

Role: friend
What I did: chatted to them on the computer
Why was it good? I like having friends
How it made me feel? good

I have lost my job.

I don't get paid any more.

I feel sad.

I would like another job.

<u>**Worksheet 4.4**</u>

Moving on

Sometimes a person with autism has unrealistic expectations about his or her future. For example, they may say things like 'I'm going to get married, have children, build a nice house and drive a fast car'. According to Vermeulen,[1] in most cases people with autism will not be able to lead a life which will include all of those things. Only a rare few individuals succeed. People with autism should not be left to feel frustrated or depressed but rather the roles that *are* open to them should be explored.

Aim: to think about what new roles the person might have, or to recycle old ones.

Objective: to move from negative feelings to positive ones.

---

1   Vermeulen, P. (2000) *I Am Special: Introducing Children and Young People to Their Autistic Spectrum Disorder.* London: Jessica Kingsley Publishers.

Exercise: Moving on

Using the circles from Worksheets 4.2 and 4.3, help the person with autism write or draw in previous and possible new roles and explore what these might mean to the person.

For example, Alan:

Role: brother
What I did: helped my younger sister
Why was it good? I like my sister
How it made me feel? good

New role: helper at local charity shop
What I do: help unpack clothes from the public
Why is it good? I see people
How does it make me feel? good

Role: friend
What I did: chatted to them on the computer
Why was it good? I like having friends
How it made me feel? good

Next, draw up a timetable of roles (the emphasis being on the role rather than the activity). The timetable does not have to be completely filled. The goal is to put some 'new roles' in. It would be beneficial to incorporate this timetable with some behavioural social skills training if necessary. We provide an example for Alan below:

Day	Monday	Tuesday	Wednesday	Thursday	Friday	Saturday	Sunday
Morning	Charity shop **'Employee'**				Cleaned house **'Cleaner'**		
Afternoon			**'Swimmer'**	Charity shop **'Employee'**			**'Cook'** for mum
Evening		Bought a pint at pub for friend **'Socializer'**				Friend for tea **'Host'**	

If for various reasons, the activities do not happen (e.g. the friend was unable to visit last time due to existing commitments), support the person to ask them again or ask someone else or have the tea anyway. This will help the person not to feel rejected and give up trying.

Odd behaviour will elicit reactions from strangers and will cause problems sooner or later. This can often lead to breakdown and loss of for example, communication, jobs and friends. Nevertheless, McConkey states that 'personal contact rather than putting people off, seems to win people over'.[1] He argues that whilst about 75 per cent of people in the community are not bothered about meeting people with disabilities, about 25 per cent are. Therefore he suggests that meetings to get to know people should take place in ordinary locations such as pubs, cafes or churches, rather than special centres. Being bullied, relationship issues and not being able to find a job are all well-known problems for people with autism. A person with autism needs to be taught how to understand people's reactions so that they are prepared for being laughed at or being turned down repeatedly or rejected again and again. This 'training' can be carried out as part of person-centred planning.

---

1   McConkey, R. (2005) 'Promoting friendships and developing social networks.' In G. Grant, P. Goward, M. Richardson and P. Ramcharan (eds) *Learning Disability: A Life Cycle Approach to Valuing people.* Maidenhead: Open University Press, p.477.

Chapter 5

Loss of Health and Wellbeing

Look to your health; and if you have it, praise God, and value it next to a good conscience; for health is the second blessing that we mortals are capable of; a blessing that money cannot buy.

Izaak Walton (1593–1683)

Introduction

Health was traditionally understood as 'absence of disease or injury'. However, the term 'health' is now regarded as a multidimensional concept. The constitution of the World Health Organization states: 'Health is a state of complete physical, mental and social wellbeing and not merely the absence of disease and infirmity'. Health then is closely linked to the concept of 'wellbeing', which is often used interchangeably with the term 'quality of life' (Felce and Perry 1995). Schalock (2004) states that wellbeing is one in a list of parts of quality of life, and Clements and Zarkowska (2000) suggest that a person who lacks wellbeing may be physically unwell and/or emotionally upset. In Figure 5.1 below, we show how health and wellbeing are interrelated with overall quality of life, using Veenhoven's (1998) typology of four aspects of wellbeing.

Whilst all individuals should be able to maximize their individual and environmental potential and embrace health (Seedhouse 1986), people on the autistic spectrum often have difficulties maintaining health and wellbeing and may need assistance to do so (Clements and Zarkowska 2000). Losing any aspect of health and wellbeing also requires individualized support. There are a variety of reasons for these difficulties, as we illustrate in this chapter by discussing each of Veenhoven's four aspects of wellbeing in relation to autism.

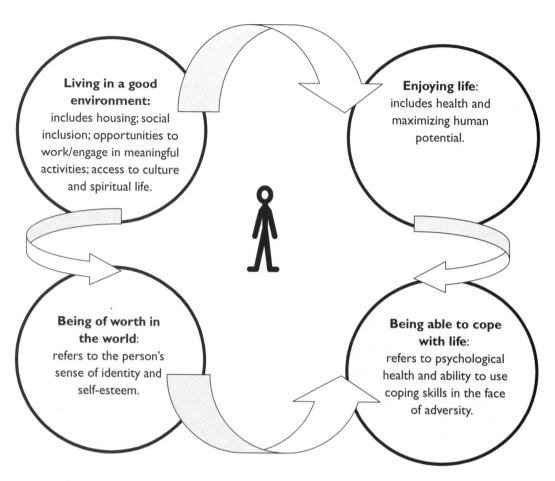

Figure 5.1 The relationship between health and wellbeing

Living in a good physical and social environment

Practical experience and research (see Chapter 2) indicates that some people with autism may live in environments which are not conducive to the maintenance of health or wellbeing. Residences may be both physically and socially isolated and individuals socially excluded, with few or limited opportunities to engage in work or meaningful activities (Ashman and Beadle-Brown 2006). Models of care or care practices may be so rigid that people with autism are prevented from exercising choice and control over their lives. When a person with autism is moved from one residence to another, they will find the loss of their old environment difficult to bear leading to behaviour which might be challenging to staff. This may come as a shock to staff where the new environment was regarded as more 'beneficial' to their client with raised expectations about outcomes.

A good environment allows individuals' spiritual and cultural needs to be met (Swinton 2004). Spirituality is a basic human right and a fundamental aspect of maintaining wellbeing. Swinton (2001) defines spirituality as a part of existence that gives humans their 'humanness' and which includes, but is not defined by, religion. Whilst we may have our own definition of spirituality, a common theme of religion and culture is their source for values, attitudes and beliefs which give meaning and importance to our lives (Hollins and Tuffrey-Wijne 2005).

Until recently, the spiritual needs of people with autism have not been explored. Webb-Mitchell (1994) argues that this is because religious communities, including churches, have continued to equate 'different' with 'deviant' and have 'betrayed people with disabilities' by disallowing them from participating within cultural and religious services and rituals (see also Chapter 6). If a neuro-typical (NT) feels that there is 'something missing in my life' they have the opportunity to seek out their own spiritual awareness using various religions or philosophies to help them. However, people with autism having similar feelings often do not have access to things which might enable them to 'find themselves'. Swinton (2001) suggests that spirituality plays a significant role in the lives of many people with intellectual and developmental disabilities, but that training is required to enable carers to recognize and support this aspect of their lives. To illustrate a case where someone's spiritual needs were not being met we return to Claire (mentioned in Chapter 2).

Case study – Claire

Claire lives in a residential home with two other people in North Wales. She has lived there for about nine years. She has autism and a mild learning disability and is wheelchair-bound. She is 41 years old. Claire's mum lives in the next village about three miles away, but when her husband had a stroke, she was no longer able to care for Claire. However, she visits Claire once a week and Claire spends a weekend at home once a month. Claire attends a local day centre twice a week, goes swimming and horse riding and has lots of photos of horses in her bedroom. After about a year living in her group home, Claire began to ask questions about the local church. She was introduced to the local Church of England when her housemates and staff went to a summer fete there. Claire showed interest in the church building and said she liked the woman vicar. One of the staff asked Claire if she thought she might like to attend. Claire was taken each Sunday morning by one of the staff for about six months. Her case files revealed that she had met a number of people, she said she liked the service and that 'she has started to talk about God's love to her and how she is going to heaven'. However, due to a reduced staffing level (one member of staff went on maternity leave and the service had difficulties replacing her), Sunday worship for Claire could no longer continue. Whilst members of the congregation had intimated that they would be willing to pick Claire up, the social care service felt that the risk to her was too great (she would need a trained carer to help her into her wheelchair). No solution was found and after three years Claire is still not attending church.

Enjoying life

In order to maximize social and employable potential, a person needs to be physically healthy even if they are physically disabled. The most common health problems in Western societies are chronic diseases – that is, degenerative illnesses such as heart disease. These diseases are referred to as lifestyle diseases because they are a result of life choices (for example smoking, not exercising, not eating a high-fibre diet) (Caltabiano and Sarafino 2002). Major advances in the health of the general population have, in part, been the result of increasing engagement in healthy behaviours encouraged by health promotion schemes.

The aim of health promotion schemes are to enable people to increase control over their health. It is difficult for people to achieve health gains and reach their health potential unless they are able to take control of the things which determine their health. By providing information and education for health and enhancing life skills, health promotion supports personal and social development. This increases the options available to people and enables them to make choices conducive to health. There are a whole range of health education, promotion and screening programmes that help to prepare people in the general population for changes in their health throughout their lifespan. Unfortunately, such resources are not always available to people with intellectual disabilities or autism, despite the increased health needs of these groups.

Loss of physical health

There is a growing body of literature on health issues and people with learning disabilities. The evidence suggests that some conditions (e.g. obesity, dental disease, gastrointestinal cancer and heart disease) are more common in older people with learning disabilities (some who may also have autism) than their peers in the general population (Evenhuis 2001). Yet even though this population seems to be at an increased risk, research suggests that the health care of people with learning disabilities is not on a par with that of the general population, particularly in relation to healthcare promotion and inclusion in screening programmes (Grant 2005). Clinical experience suggests that the same is true for people on the autistic spectrum.

The American Association on Mental Retardation (AAMR) states in its Declaration on Health Parity for Persons with Intellectual and Developmental Disabilities that 'all people with Intellectual and Developmental Disabilities should have a health plan that is ongoing throughout a person's life and crosses all settings; this plan should begin with a proactive assessment of health risks, needs and supports'.

In the UK *Valuing People: A New Strategy for Learning Disability for the 21st Century* (DoH 2001b) introduced the notion of 'health facilitators' and 'health action planning'. The health facilitator (a member of the local community learning disability team, usually the learning disability nurse) is responsible for supporting the person with learning disabilities to access the care they need from primary care and other NHS services. Health action plans are completed by health facilitators in partnership with other primary care practitioners. The action plan is part of the person-centred plan and includes details of needs in, for example, dental care, fitness, vision, mobility, nutrition, exercise and medication.

People with autism often have difficulties with planning, imagining the future and making choices. This will affect *how* health planning is done, but it should not affect *whether* it is done.

Autism is a complex condition, the biological causes of which are still poorly understood (see Chapter 1). It is clear that there are multiple genetic and environmental factors, and a significant amount of research has been conducted in an attempt to clarify how these factors impact on the 'symptoms' of autism. The complex and fascinating nature of autism has resulted in an intense interest by the medical field; but even so, little research has been conducted on the healthcare of autistic people. The research that has been conducted in relation to health has tended to focus on the prevalence of various medical conditions in this population. Below is a brief summary of this research.

- Some studies have indicated that there is an increased likelihood that people with autism and a learning disability may suffer from coexisting medical conditions such as epilepsy (Gillberg and Billstedt 2000).

- Chronic gastrointestinal disturbances, including diarrhoea, constipation and abdominal discomfort, have been reported in a significant proportion of children diagnosed with autism (Roberts *et al.* 2001).

- There is increasing evidence of an association between the immune system and autism (Molloy *et al.* 2006).

- Research on the mental health of people on the spectrum has demonstrated that people with autistic spectrum conditions (ASCs) may be more susceptible than the general population to minor stressful life events because any subsequent changes to their lifestyle may interfere with their rituals and obsessions (Tsakanikos *et al.* 2007). Furthermore, a study by Leyer *et al.* (2006) indicated that children on the spectrum often meet the diagnostic criteria for more than one coexisting psychiatric disorder. Many people on the autistic spectrum report high levels of fear and anxiety. For example, Temple Grandin once described herself as 'living in a constant state of fear' (Grandin 1995).

The anxiety issue is an important one. In order to function effectively, a calm, alert state is required. If we are in a constant state of anxiety, our learning and performance is impeded. Anxiety is closely linked to the adrenal glands. When we are stressed or anxious, the adrenal glands release the hormones adrenaline and cortisol. As these stress hormones flood our body, our heart rate and blood pressure increases, oxygen flows to the muscles and non-essential functions like digestion are put on hold. These biochemical effects are useful for emergency situations (i.e. fight or flight), and when the situation has calmed down our body returns to a normal state. However, if we are in a constant state of anxiety, our body is subjected to elevated levels of adrenaline for long periods of time. The body does not have a chance to recover and this can lead to damage to the heart and arteries. Exhausted adrenal glands means a reduction in the efficiency of the immune system, resulting in a loss of health. Clinical experience seems to indicate that a loss of health due to adrenal gland fatigue is something that people on the autistic spectrum are at an increased risk of.

Health promotion and people on the autistic spectrum

As mentioned earlier, health promotion focuses on ensuring that there are equal opportunities and resources to enable all people to achieve their fullest health potential. Unfortunately, little attention has been given to making sure the necessary resources are made available and are user-friendly for the autistic population. Gates (1986) identifies three levels of prevention that must be addressed so as to maintain and promote the health of individuals with learning disabilities. This model is also useful when considering the health care of people with ASCs.

LEVEL 1: ACTIONS TAKEN TO PREVENT HEALTH LOSS BEFORE IT OCCURS

Health education concerning prevention of chronic diseases by living a healthy lifestyle tends not to be taught formally to people on the autistic spectrum. Due to difficulties with communication and sensory processing, autistic people are also not always able to access information on healthy living through the media. Learning about different lifestyles is what NT people do through friendships but often people on the spectrum do not experience close friendships (see Chapter 2) and hence do not learn from their peer group either.

Good nutritional and exercise habits are lifelong investments, but experience shows that many people on the spectrum have difficulty seeing the 'cause and effect' relationship. Issues like nutritional management can be too complicated or inaccessible for some people with ASCs who may have problems eating a wide range of foods due to their sensory issues. These problems can be compounded if they rely on other people who have limited nutritional knowledge to prepare their meals.

LEVEL 2: ACTIONS RELATED TO EARLY DETECTION OF HEALTH LOSS

Sensory issues can cause problems in relation to screening programmes and physical examinations. People with autism may feel unable to undergo examinations at a hospital where bright lights, machinery humming and large groups of other patients can cause much anxiety. A need for extra resources, more support and longer appointments is something which economic pressures often prevent.

LEVEL 3: ACTIONS TAKEN TO AVOID NEEDLESS PROGRESSION OF HEALTH LOSS

Changes in health tend to result in a dawning realization that one is no longer able to do certain things. This can mean that there is a need to make changes to our daily routine which might even include a move to a new environment. This can result in extreme increases in anxiety for people on the spectrum. Palliative care professionals have for many years maintained that the best way to enable people to cope with a loss of health is to be open and honest about its consequences (Grant *et al.* 2005). This tends not to happen for people with autism as those who support them sometimes feel that this kind of information would cause an extreme increase in anxiety. Such increases in anxiety can result in behaviour that is difficult to manage. However, there is a need for people on the spectrum to be given at least basic information about the specific health condition and rationales for any changes to their lifestyle. If information is consistent and they are frequently reminded in a way they can tolerate, it can help them to comply with any changes they need to make.

Good practice to help manage loss of health

Providing choices about what treatment or care the individual would prefer is critical if the best possible quality of life is to be maintained. If the person concerned is not informed or involved in the process then this is impossible to achieve (Grant *et al.* 2005). Below are some suggestions that highlight good practice in supporting someone on the autistic spectrum who is experiencing a loss of health.

- There is a need to assess the person's understanding of the illness, as this could affect the way he or she copes with it. It needs to be discussed in concrete terms by talking about observable symptoms and behaviour, rather than explanations of its underlying cause. The person's own vocabulary should be used and answers to questions should be simple and based on the truth.

- It will be important to bear in mind any previous negative experience of medical intervention or hospitalization.

- It may be necessary to establish whether anyone in the patient's social circle has had a similar illness or to explain that this illness is not necessarily the same as others.

- Where appropriate, health planning should be completed as part of the individual's person-centred plan.

- It is important to keep up with routine appointments as a way of familiarizing the individual with the healthcare professional and the environment. If the person is used to routine visits, they will be more likely to cope with a visit in an emergency.

- Prepare the person for visits to healthcare professionals by talking them through (perhaps with the aid of pictures) what will happen. It is of course important to balance this against overloading the person with information, which could result in them obsessing about the visit.

- Familiarize the person with specific equipment (e.g. blood pressure cuff) before the visit. If appropriate, let them watch the procedure being carried out on someone else (e.g. family member/staff/nurse) before it is done on them.

- Schedule appointments so as to cut down on waiting time (e.g. first appointment for the clinic). If the waiting room is going to cause problems because of too many people or bright lights, ask if there is another room you can wait in (such as a spare doctor's office or examination room).

- Keep a record of changes in behaviour, symptoms and medications. This is particularly important for people with an ASC who have limited communication skills and who find it difficult to express how they are feeling.

- Teach healthcare within general everyday activities (e.g. cooking healthy meals).

Being/feeling of worth in the world

Feeling that you are of worth in the world or having high self-esteem is dependent upon feeling socially included (see Chapter 4). If you are excluded from society and discriminated against, you struggle to develop good social networks and engage in meaningful activities (see Chapter 2). As a result, your sense of identity and self-esteem can be compromised (Clements 2005). To feel of worth in the world, individuals with autism need people who will respect and think well of them. Self-esteem is also related to having some control over self or, as Rutter (1984, p.60) states, 'a feeling of your own self-worth, as well as a feeling that you can deal with things, that you can control what happens to you...one important quality is a feeling that you are in fact master of your own destiny'. This is not the experience of many people on the autistic spectrum.

There are a number of risk factors associated with low self-esteem, such as communication difficulties, discrimination and difficulty adapting to new situations. Arguably, people with autism tend to have more risk factors in their profiles than NTs. Amongst other things, they have problems with effective social competence, learning new skills and generalizing their learning to new environments as well as problem solving. As a result, many people on the autistic spectrum suffer with low self-esteem and reduced emotional wellbeing as illustrated in the following case study.

Case study – Christine

Christine is 33 years old. For a long period in her adult life she lived in a residential home with three other people who were also all on the autistic spectrum. Christine is able to interact using verbal communication, but staff at the home often overestimated how much she understood. As a result, Christine often got things wrong, and because staff thought she understood they assumed she was getting things wrong on purpose or that she was for some reason trying to annoy them. Years of living in this situation did a great deal of damage to Christine's self-esteem. As her self-esteem deteriorated so did her sense of wellbeing. As a result her obsessive and ritualistic behaviours increased. A vicious circle was created whereby the more obsessive and ritualistic behaviours Christine exhibited, the more annoyed and frustrated staff became. Naturally this led to further decreases in her self-esteem. Christine was eventually admitted to hospital with severe depression.

Ability to cope with life

One of the biggest issues for people on the autistic spectrum and their ability to cope with everyday life is the difficulty they have with information-processing. People on the autistic spectrum can only process one bit of information at a time, which means that they are constantly missing bits and trying to fill in the gaps. If you can process what someone is saying but not process their body movements or facial expressions at the same time, then it is easy to misunderstand the meaning of what is being said to you. The energy it takes trying to make sense of the world and the anxiety it causes results in being vulnerable to a loss of psychological wellbeing (Williams 2006).

Detection of a loss of wellbeing can be problematic, as people with autism will find it difficult to monitor and identify their feelings. As their sense of wellbeing deteriorates, the person will become less and less tolerant. It is likely that the person will want to isolate themselves and engage in ever-increasing ritualistic behaviour. This will provide a way of cutting down on the need to process information as the repetitive motion always has the same outcome. The person with autism will also suffer from increased levels of sensory sensitivity, and they will be at increased risk of losing control. Often people on the spectrum have developed some good coping skills for managing their anxiety in the form of obsessive or ritualistic behaviours, but their ways of coping are not always recognized by those who support them, as illustrated by the following case study.

Case study – Peter

Peter is ten years old and attends his local special needs school. The school is not autism-specific, and as a result the staff are not very knowledgeable about autism. Observing Peter it was clear that he had enormous difficulty coping with the sensory environment in his classroom. He seemed to find the fluorescent lights painful and would constantly screw his eyes shut. He continually had his fingers in his ears as if the noise was too much for him, and he physically withdrew when anyone touched his shoulder or arms (which the classroom assistant constantly did). Peter had developed two clear ways of coping with the classroom environment. The first was that when things got too much he would sign 'toilet'. This would result in the classroom assistant escorting him to the toilet, where Peter could experience a couple of minutes' peace and quiet. On occasions Peter would sign 'toilet' every five to ten minutes, and when staff realized that Peter was not always using the toilet when he got there, they started to refuse to take him every time he asked. On these occasions the only way left for Peter to get some peace and quiet was to become physically aggressive so that he was removed from the classroom.

The second method that Peter had developed to cope with his environment was to engage in the repetitive behaviour of rocking in an effort to block out all the other incoming sensory information. Staff interpreted this as Peter not wanting to engage in his school work. They therefore prevented him from rocking by sitting him on a chair against a wall and then placing the table so that there was no room to rock. Once again, when things got too painful, the only option left to Peter was physical aggression.

Fact Sheet 5.1

Loss of health and wellbeing

Everyone should be able to maximize their individual and

environmental potential and have good health.

But, if you have autism you may have difficulties maintaining

health and wellbeing and you may need help to do so.

Clinical experience seems to indicate that a loss of health

due to adrenal gland fatigue is something that people on the autistic spectrum are at an increased risk of.

Sensory issues can cause problems in relation to

screening programmes and physical examinations.

If you have autism you may feel unable to undergo examinations

at a hospital because of bright lights, machinery humming

too many other patients.

This can all cause anxiety.

Good practice in relation to health and wellbeing

People with autism need to:

- be fully involved in person-centred planning to maximize

- choice and control over their own lives

- have access to appropriate housing

- be provided with opportunities to engage in meaningful activities

- have their spiritual and cultural needs assessed and met

- be supported to develop social and sexual relationships

- have regular health checks, exercise and high-fibre diet

- be supported to develop more coping skills.

Staff need to devise ways of recording

and regularly reviewing a person's sense of wellbeing

so that they can detect at an early stage when it begins to deteriorate.

When it is detected that an individual's sense of wellbeing is deteriorating

interventions must be implemented immediately.

Worksheet 5.1

Identifying signs and symptoms of loss of health and wellbeing

Aim: to help staff look for and identify any signs and symptoms of loss of health and wellbeing.

Objective: to enable individuals with autism to get the right type and level of support they need to ensure maintenance of health and wellbeing.

Exercise: Identifying signs and symptoms of loss of health and wellbeing

Symptoms of a lack of wellbeing may involve one or more of the following:

1. A diagnosable physical health problem such as throat or ear infection.
2. A sense that the person is 'under the weather'.
3. The emotions the person expresses are mainly anger, distress, anxiety, sadness.
4. The person repeatedly talks about how no one likes him/her, what a failure he/she is, etc.
5. The person dwells on bad memories.
6. The person has poor concentration, an inability to settle, muscular tension, etc. due to a constant state of anxiety.
7. The person continually seeks reassurance about what is happening, who is around, when particular events will occur, specific worries.
8. Sleep disturbance.
9. Appetite change.
10. Reduced tolerance to the physical environment (noise, heat, crowding, etc.) and social environment.
11. Increased compulsive/obsessive behaviour.
12. Increases in the frequency or intensity of aggression, self-injury, and property damage.
13. Withdrawal from activities.
14. Unwillingness to accept any limits being set.
15. Loss of skills.
16. A clear and diagnosable depression.[1]

1 Clements, J. and Zarkowska, E. (2000) *Behavioural Concerns and Autistic Spectrum Disorders: Explanations and Strategies for Change*. London: Jessica Kingsley Publishers, p.119.

Worksheet 5.2

Sharing feelings diary

Aim: to support the person to monitor their own feelings throughout the day.

Objective: to help individuals identify and express appropriately how they feel about their own health and wellbeing.

Exercise: Sharing feelings diary

People on the autistic spectrum find it difficult to process information from the world around them whilst also processing their internal state. One way of helping people to take some time out of their day to monitor their feelings is by encouraging them to engage with a diary.

As with many of the exercises there is no one way of doing this and it will depend on the communication skills of the person involved. It could be a written diary with some prompt questions to help the person to know what to write about.

We give an example from Tom's diary below:

An extract from Tom's diary

Monday	My feelings
Morning	8am staff woke me up. It was snowing so the bus made me late to work and I was cross.
Afternoon	Mike took me shopping. We had a pint in the pub. I like going out with Mike.
Tuesday	Didn't do much today. I was bored
Morning	Had a lie in today coz no work. I hate the snow.
Afternoon	Mandy made dinner with me. She doesn't like me. She never smiles.
Wednesday	Gave Sarah my clothes to wash. She wanted me to help wash them but I didn't want to. I was angry with her.
Morning	Went to college today. Saw Ben at college. We ate lunch together. Ben is my friend. I like college.
Afternoon	Travelled home on the bus. Some kids called me names. I shouted at them. No one likes me.

To help with the diary, you could use the following prompt questions:

- What did you do today?
- What things made you happy today?
- Did anything make you angry, sad or frightened today?

Alternatively, the diary could simply be a sheet with faces on it showing different expressions and the person ticks which face expresses how they are feeling at that point in time.

We give an example below:

Tick ✓ how you are feeling

My feelings						

Monday

Morning

Afternoon

Tuesday

Morning

Afternoon

Wednesday

Morning

Afternoon

Or the diary could be a video recording where on a regular basis the person with autism chats to the video recorder about how they are feeling. Another version of this would be to have regular face-to-face or telephone chats with a trusted person to discuss their thoughts and feelings.

Note

In our experience carers often attempt to avoid discussing feelings with those they support because of difficulties of managing behavioural responses which may occur. In some cases discussions may need to be limited both in terms of time and who such discussions take place with. However, it is important that the person is supported to express how they are feeling in appropriate ways. Having a structured time and place to share their feelings will help the person to feel listened to, something we all need if our sense of wellbeing is to be maintained.

Worksheet 5.3

Feeling well! Moving towards a more healthy lifestyle

Aim: to introduce practical strategies for helping an individual improve their sense of health and wellbeing.

Objective: to enable individuals who have lost a part of their health and/or wellbeing to move towards a better quality of life.

Exercise: Feeling well!
Moving towards a more healthy lifestyle

1. Living in a good environment

Social support

See Worksheet 2.3.

Engagement in activities

A person's lifestyle should centre on engaging in preferred activities and experiencing success. You should get an idea about what a person likes from conducting the activity taster sessions described in Worksheet 4.1. Once you know what a person likes to do and where their strengths lie, activities that match this should be structured into their day. Individual activities should be short and there should be a focus on 'little and often'.[1]

Spiritual/cultural wellbeing

These suggestions can be used in relation to any religion or culture, not just Christianity.

- Research has demonstrated that friendship is the main way in which people express their spirituality and have their spiritual needs met.[2] Support the person to develop friendships – see Worksheet 2.3.

- Initiate contact with local faith communities. Prepare them to meet the person you support by discussing communication methods.

- Discuss the practicalities of attending a worship service, e.g. where can you take the person with autism should they become distressed during the service? Where would it be best for the person to sit? Can they come in late and leave or miss parts of the service due to sensory issues, such as loud music, bells, smell of incense, etc?

- Arrange for the person with autism to visit the venue so they can get used to it. Do this initially when no one else is there.

- Allow the person to take with them any object which they can use to keep calm and hence enhance their experience. This could be some form of 'twiddle', such as a rubber band or string; it might be an object of visual focus, such as a book. Items that provide comfort and security at home might be made available at the place of worship.

- Try to encourage multiple friendships and acquaintances by rotating peer escorts.

- Use extra visual cues such as pictures during readings that tell a story.

- Encourage the person to have a role, such as handing out prayer books.

---

1   Mansell, J. and Beadle-Brown, J. (2004) 'Person-centred planning or person-centred action? Policy and practice in intellectual disability services.' *Journal of Applied Research in Intellectual Disabilities* 17, 1, 1–9.

2   Swinton, J. and Powrie, E. (2004) *Why Are We Here? Meeting the Spiritual Needs of People with Learning Disabilities.* London: Mental Health Foundation.

- Support the person to have a role in the community by volunteering to assist in the delivery of cards or food to homebound individuals, etc.

- Involve the person in preparing for and celebrating occasions that are special to them, their family, culture and religion. Support the person to participate in the rituals associated with the occasion.

- Celebrating is about being thankful for the good things in your life and feeling part of a group. Support the person to have a meal or party with friends and family.

- We all need 'quiet' time. Support the individual to find space and time to sit and reflect or simply experience a state of tranquillity and calmness.

2. Enjoying life

People on the autistic spectrum are not always going to have the skills to express whether they are enjoying life or not. We also have a tendency to record incidents of behaviour that challenge us rather than how often someone displays behaviour that suggests they are happy. It can sometimes be more useful to record how often a person smiles than it can be to record how often a person screams. In the same vein it is useful to design interventions that focus on increasing the smiling behaviour, rather than focusing on decreasing the screaming behaviour.

Physical health

Draw up a Health Action Plan that will ensure that the person has their health needs met including the opportunity for regular health checks with the doctor, dentist and optician.

e.g. Health Action Plan for Rosalind for next five months:

January	February	March	April	May
Visit doctor to review blood pressure Visit chiropodist	Meeting with community nurse to discuss how I could be supported to have regular checks for lumps in my breasts	Visit chiropodist	Visit dentist	Visit chiropodist

To help the individual understand any illnesses or visits to healthcare professionals it may be useful to use one of the packs that are available such as the pack called 'Feeling Poorly'.[3] The pack has pictorial representations of different illness and types of pain in the form of symbols and line drawings. Speech therapy services are also developing general practitioner packs for doctors, with symbols and signs to facilitate better communication between people with learning disabilities and their GPs. Some such packs may be useful when working with a person with autism. Finally, there is a 'Going into Hospital' picture book which is part of the 'Books Beyond Words' series developed by Sheila Hollins (www.rcpsych.ac.uk/publications/booksbeyondwords.aspx). It has a series of

---

3   Dodd, K. and Gathard, J. (1998) *Feeling Poorly*. Brighton: Pavilion.

pictures depicting a planned admission and an emergency admission, and can be used with or without the accompanying story.

Physical exercise

Regular, structured aerobic exercise that builds fitness makes a positive contribution to emotional and physical wellbeing. The key is to find an activity which the person enjoys and that can become part of their lifestyle.

It is important to follow intense phases of exercise with cool-down periods to avoid the risk of problematic behaviour associated with heightened arousal.

Ensure that the exercise is structured. Unstructured exercise can lead to increases in excitability, with no benefit to emotional wellbeing.

Use special interests to increase the motivation to exercise.

3. Being of worth in the world

Self-esteem

According to Mruk,[4] self-esteem is accepting and valuing yourself whilst doing things competently and in a way you find morally acceptable. Below are some suggestions about how to increase a person's self-esteem based on the above definition.

- Give the person positive feedback about both their value and their competence, e.g. tell them when they do things well, demonstrate that their opinion matters by listening and acting upon it. If you give someone five times the amount of positive feedback compared to negative feedback, you will increase or at least maintain their self-esteem.

- Make the expectations placed on a person clear, consistent and achievable.

- Support the person to put together a list of things that they have achieved that they can refer to when they are feeling low.

- Celebrate successes.

- With input from the person themselves (and if appropriate those in their circle of support) identify what the person's dreams are. We all have dreams, and dreams are very important in motivating us to engage in life. Some of us will reach our dreams, some of us won't, and some of us will decide they aren't what we wanted once we get them, but we all have dreams and we all try to work towards them. It is important that we support someone with autism to visualize their dreams and identify the steps they need to take in trying to achieve those dreams. The steps need to be achievable even if the ultimate aim seems unrealistic.

- Support the person to spruce up their personal appearance, e.g. go shopping for new clothes, get a haircut, have nails done, put on some aftershave, etc.

---

4   Mruk, C. (1999) *Self Esteem: Research, Theory and Practice.* London: Free Association Books.

4. Being able to cope with life

Relaxation

Clinical experience suggests that many people with ASC have difficulty achieving a relaxed state, but if they are assisted to do so, this can help their sense of wellbeing. Below are some guidelines for conducting a relaxation session:

1. Get the person to sit or lie, rather than stand or move about.

2. Reduce external stimulus (e.g. minimum noise and lowered lighting levels).

3. Use a dominant repetitive stimulus (e.g. music, chanting).

4. Although many people with autism are sensitive to touch, they often respond well to massage and acupressure.

5. Teach steady and controlled breathing. Try using balloons, bubbles, windmills or musical instruments to help the person learn how to take steady breaths and slowly breathe out.

6. Use massage if appropriate.

7. During the sessions introduce a distinctive, highly portable cue to signal the start of the session (e.g. a particular word, a special picture, a distinctive aroma). Over time the cue itself may come to be associated with a relaxed state. It can then be made available in the person's everyday environments and used to help 'on the spot' calming when the person starts to become tense.

8. For people with chronic and pervasive anxiety it may be necessary to schedule several sessions a day if a meaningful impact upon functioning is to be made.

Chapter 6

Loss Through Death

I don't really understand what death is and I wasn't allowed to go to my mum's funeral because they said I was acting silly.

Francis Jones – a person with autism

Introduction

Death of a loved one is possibly the most acute loss most people will experience in a lifetime. Such a loss can trigger a reaction called *grief* which describes the multiple feelings and emotions of deep sorrow expressed in a set of psychological and physiological behaviours which we call *mourning* (Stroebe *et al.* 1993). These behaviours might include public expressions of grief (e.g. crying or wailing) which are influenced by cultural, religious and family norms and values. *Grieving* is the state of feeling grief and the *bereavement period* is the time span or episode during which grieving occurs (Worden 1991). The bereavement period can take years, and there is increased risk of psychiatric problems following bereavement when people are not supported to grieve or given adequate consideration or sensitive treatment (Oswain 1985, 1991; Raji and Hollins 2003). In Chapter 1 of this resource we illustrated how people might go through interrelated stages of grief although not necessarily in any particular order. In this chapter we discuss how we might support people with autism who are grieving.

Whilst people with autism will experience specific difficulties associated with the death of a loved one, issues general to both neuro-typicals (NTs) and people with learning disabilities are also relevant to people with autistic spectrum conditions (ASC). Since there is virtually no literature on bereavement and autism we refer first to the research in the general population and on learning disability to inform us of these issues.

Grief, the general population and people with learning disabilities

The complex issues of death and bereavement in relation to the general population and people with learning disabilities have traditionally tended to be professionalized or ignored (Cambridge *et al.* 1994), possibly because the topic is a sensitive one. Yet, due to advancements in medicine and, some would say, better quality of living and care, longevity beyond national retirement age has become increasingly common among people with learning disabilities (Bigby 2004; Grant 2005), with an average increase of 30–40 years (Cooke 1997; Jancar 1990). Thus, individuals are often living to experience not only the death of friends in their school, college, clubs, work and day centre context but also their relatives and parents (Hollins and Tuffrey-Wijne 2005). It is little wonder then that issues of death and bereavement have recently emerged as powerful experiences in the lives of people with learning disabilities and ones which they want to talk about (Schwabenland 1999). However, Blackman (2003) recounts how many people who have experienced un-acknowledged and unsupported loss exhibit challenging behaviour and end up in secure and forensic units. Blackman advocates that residential and support staff, other than trained bereavement counsellors, should acquire the knowledge of the specific needs and experiences of people who are suffering a loss.

Being left out of important death rituals

Religious and cultural rituals invest death with meaning. In some cultures, funeral rites also provide a social sanction for the outward expression of grief (Martinson, Deck and Adams 1992). Sheldon (1998) argues that repeated explanations and supported involvement in funeral rituals (such as funeral attendance or visits to the grave) have been shown to reduce repetitive questions about where the dead person is, and subsequent challenging behaviour. Non-participation in rituals can delay the grieving process (Cathcart 1994a, 1994b, 1994c) and deny the person potential social support from networks of relation-ships (Taylor 1980). Nevertheless, many people with learning disabilities (and people with an ASC) are left out of the rituals of death and dying (Blackman 2003), including planning and organizing the funeral. Raji and Hollins (2003) interviewed funeral directors and rep-resentatives from six religious groups in a multicultural inner London borough only to find a lack of involvement of people with learning disabilities in funeral rites.

What about my own funeral?

Whether and how individuals with learning disabilities and people with ASC are ade-quately and appropriately supported to express preferences and make choices about the type of funeral *they* would like when they die are important life course considerations; but in practice, opportunities for these are sporadic across and within agencies (Cambridge *et al.* 2001). A recent study in which 16 people with learning disabilities were asked what they thought about death and funerals (Forrester-Jones 2004) revealed that individuals had many questions concerning their own funeral, and these related to questions concern-ing belief and spirituality. However, no studies were found which examined the views of people with autism about death and funerals. Botsford and King (2005) suggest that in the general population, people are increasingly wishing to purchase 'pre-need' funerals, and write 'advance directives' (living wills) that clearly state end-of-life care preferences and wishes. It seems that people with learning disabilities are not yet being given these choices. Self-advocacy groups such as Not Dead Yet argue that this is another example of the effect of prejudicial and dehumanizing social attitudes concerning the quality of life and death of people with disabilities (Kitching 1987; Singer 1994). They point out how devaluing attitudes such as the belief that living with a disability is a 'fate worse than death' may encourage the withdrawal of treatment or the physician-assisted suicide of a person with a disability in the guise of promoting the 'right to die' or 'death with dignity' (Johnson 2003; Taylor cited in Botsford and King 2005). There is clearly a need for training of care-givers in this area in the UK. In New Jersey, a five-day course on 'End of Life and Palliative Care' is now provided for all state guardians of people with disabilities which includes social workers and support staff (Botsford and King 2005).

Service and professional support in relation to funerals

Policy (including Valuing People: A New Strategy for Learning Disability for the 21st Century (2001)), the first White Paper on learning disabilities for 30 years has been silent on the issue of death and people with learning disabilities. A Department of Health funded longitudinal study on community care (Cambridge et al. 2001; Cambridge et al. 2002; Forrester-Jones et al. 2002) investigated outcomes and costs of over 200 people with learning disabilities. Whilst not a specified area of investigation, unsolicited discussions with managers of homes and services revealed confusion and uncertainty over issues surrounding death and bereavement in general, and in particular over responsibility for the organization and payment of clients' funerals. In some of the London borough services, private schemes had been set up for residents, with monthly payments contributing to clients' own coffin and funeral. However, it was unclear to what extent clients had given informed consent to participate in these schemes.

Ramirez et al. (1995), Phillips and Cuthill (2002) and Ptacek and Ellison (2000) all argue that professionals may find it difficult to support people who are bereaved because they feel they are not trained adequately to help individuals understand and cope with the finality of death. In particular, professionals have reported the following fears about their own abilities to support people who are bereaved:

- fear of causing pain (contrary to the caring role) (Buckman 1992; Read 1998)

- fear of being blamed for the death; Hollins (1993) argues that there is nearly always a projection of feelings from bereaved individuals onto professionals

- fear of admitting that they do not know why someone has died (Read 1998)

- fear of saying the wrong things (Read 1998)

- fear of an unpredictable emotional response and reaction leading to challenging behaviour

- fear of being ineffectual and unable to deal with the client's expectations (e.g. of a cure for a fatally ill parent)

- fear of displaying their own emotions (Buckman 1992)

- fear of the burden of care which may seem overwhelming and compounded when a person requires palliative care (Todd 2005)

- fear that acceptance of support from outside agencies might undermine their caring commitments (Brown, Burns and Flynn 2002).

McKechnie (2006) argues that the way in which individuals cope with grief and dying varies according to the experiences and understanding of their carers. Therefore, if the fears of support staff mentioned above are not dealt with, it is less likely that the person with autism will be able to cope with grief and dying.

Palliative care and death

Cancer, respiratory and vascular diseases are now the most common causes of death for older disabled adults (Patja 2001). However, there is little research on how these are managed in palliative care (Tuffrey-Wijne 2003; Todd and Blackman 2005). Brown *et al.* (2002) and Todd (2002) argue that disability services find it difficult to face the transition of people in their care from living to dying since (a) services have been working towards bringing 'social death' to an end and therefore 'death' of people with learning disabilities is difficult to bear, and (b) their job is to keep people physically well. This might explain in part why few people with learning disabilities are accessing specialist palliative care services (Brown *et al.* 2002; McEnhill 2004). Rather, staff tend to struggle on with support from the GP or district nurse. Todd (2005) further argues that staff have reported being un-prepared for what dying might entail and tend to be reluctant to place people who are dying in hospitals. Hospital staff are often perceived by support workers as uncaring and unsympathetic to people with learning disabilities, and death in hospital is viewed as 'not a good death' (Todd 2005). Carers' fears may be well grounded since diagnosis of cancer in people with learning disabilities has often been found to be delayed and treatment provided unnecessarily or differently compared to non-disabled patients (Botsford 2004). Todd (2005) and Oliver, Forrester-Jones and Duplock (2007) suggest that improved communication and understanding between different professions is needed.

Todd (2005) also found that staff had difficulties with informing people who were dying of their prognosis, and showed a reluctance to involve or provide opportunities for individuals to talk about their own dying. Botsford and King (2005) reported that residential staff were apprehensive about how to support surviving residents, being anxious about what to say and do. They also found few references, guidelines or resources on providing bereavement support to people with learning disabilities, staff or family, compared to the literature on the general population.

Whilst a life-cycle approach to care is now applied in research and practice with individuals with learning disabilities, end-of-life issues continue to be least studied. It is only in the last 15–20 years that resources on end-of-life care for older people with learning disabilities have appeared (Botsford 2000; Wadsworth and Harper 1991; Yanok and Beifus 1993). Yet, at the time of writing, we know of only one specialist learning disability bereavement and loss service in the UK, the ROC Loss and Bereavement Service (Blackman 1999). Noelle Blackman also heads up a specialist learning disability bereavement service in Hertfordshire, UK. There is also the National Network for the Palliative Care of People with Learning Disabilities (McEnhill 2006), made up of partnerships between palliative care professionals, people working in learning disability services and carers. Its main aim is to encourage palliative and healthcare professionals and learning disability professionals to find positive ways of working in partnership. In the US, the Robert Wood Johnson Foundation funds community–state partnerships to improve end-of-life care for people with learning disabilities. However, each state has developed its own policies and procedures which may or may not include shared Medicaid payments for the service provider and the hospice agency. The inadequacy of the payment structure sometimes forces hospice care to be delayed or denied.

Physical and emotional symptoms

Breathlessness, lack of appetite, a body temperature drop and pain can be responsible for the beginning or relapse of another illness (see Hollins and Sireling 1989). Hollins and Sireling (1999) advise that warm drinks, sleep and a stable routine can help. Psychological and emotional symptoms may cause physical pain, loss of skills including incontinence and mobility difficulties resulting in increased dependency. Some individuals will experience very frightening nightmares and may need someone to wake them up, give them a warm milky drink and sit with them for a while. Assessments should be avoided at these times since they would give a false reading.

If some people do not appear to grieve a loss (Brelstaff 1984), this could be delayed shock (Kitching 1987). Some individuals will ask: Should I feel sad? How sad should I feel? Shall I cry? Others may react by giggling at the bedside of a dying person or at the funeral, reflecting uncertainty or misunderstanding at what is happening.

Grief issues specific to people with autism

As already mentioned, there is virtually no literature on the subject of grief, bereavement and autism. Two surveys focused on the reactions of people with autism who had experienced the loss of a loved one, and the strategies staff developed to support them (Allison 1992; Rawlings 2000). Based on these surveys the National Autistic Society (Allison 2001) issued the following guidance:

- Each person with autism will react individually to bereavement and the approach to support needs to be as unique as the individual involved.

- People with autism may share the common responses to death and bereavement such as denial, anger and despair.

- The grieving processes of people with autism are profoundly affected by their disabilities.

- Skilled support is an important factor in helping individuals move through their grief.

It is therefore difficult to generalize the ways in which people with autism will experience loss through death, but such a loss may give rise to any of the primary difficulties we have described in previous chapters, linked to the stages of grief provided in Chapter 1 of this resource. These include phobias, fears, obsession, lack of understanding, and resistance to change, which can be considered by others to be inappropriate reactions or even callous in-difference. People with an ASC, whose senses define their experiences of physical contact with others and with objects, depend on the security of familiarity. This may be affected by someone dying. Because of the difficulties in finding words to express emotions, farewell rituals are important. They go through a process of bereavement similar to a person with a learning disability but tend to be more impulsive in their reactions.

When a person close to someone with an ASC dies, it is not always easy to know how much to tell them. If they think they have been given too much or too little information, they might not be able to voice their concerns or ask the right questions. In this situation there is a high risk that the individual will develop clinical anxiety and/or depression (Maguire 1998). A person with autism should be referred to a professional to address be-reavement (e.g. a bereavement counsellor, community nurse or psychologist from a community learning disability team) if:

- they deny that anyone has died, or act as if nothing has happened

- they threaten or talk of suicide (this is a particularly difficult issue since many people with autism suffer from depression and may generally have thoughts of suicide)

- they become unusually and persistently aggressive or engage in anti-social behaviour

- they become withdrawn and socially isolated.

Who the deceased was, how and why they died, the closeness of the relationship, the role they played in the individual's life, previous experiences of grief, unresolved grief and de-pression all have a bearing on a person's reactions to a death (Worden 1991). Just like for NTs, natural deaths are usually more easily accepted than accidental deaths, suicides and murders, which are particularly difficult to bear for people with autism.

People with autism might also think they caused the death of someone else by their own actions. Guilt is anger turned in on oneself, and people need reassurance that no one could stop the death and that it wasn't anyone's fault. Anxiety, fear and panic will be heightened in people with autism, not only because of losing someone significant who may have represented stability and security, but also because any change is threatening. The death of a loved one may also give rise to fear of their own death, fear of going to sleep, or fear that other family members may die. People with autism may also feel intense despair or emptiness.

Social support

For people who may have a very limited number of close relationships (see Chapter 2) the death of a friend or family member may be catastrophic, and re-investing in other people is very difficult if you don't have many options. Individuals may also become highly dependent on members of staff, who might be unable to offer long-term emotional care or support. People with autism may not have the self-awareness, motivation or experience to seek helpful activities and they often cannot have access to them without help from carers. In the absence of meaningful activities, they may turn to undesirable habits or obsessions as a source of comfort, this behaviour persisting long after the period of grieving is over. They will also be unlikely to have an expectation and comfort in the fact that the emotional and physical pain they are suffering will eventually come to an end. On the other hand, we have experienced cases where people with autism have movingly offered comfort to relatives and friends who are bereaved.

The role of the main carer (could be key worker, support worker or family member) is important in supporting the bereaved person with autism throughout the process. This can be a difficult role since the client's needs may not always correspond with the duty rota. However, if social support is provided at the start of loss, many of the complications which occur within grief may be pre-empted. It is important that support staff attempt not only to support the person with autism to achieve a successful resolution of grief, but also to transform their experiences into an opportunity for growth. To be able to do this the National Autistic Society in the UK advises that staff should know how the deceased looked, their personality, the nature of the relationship and activities shared. Staff should also be aware of the grieving process and how to undertake the practical arrangements sur-rounding bereavement. Person-centred planning is an accepted way of working with people with autism to find out what is important in their lives and to enable them to make choices. Conversations about end-of-life wishes should therefore be incorporated into such planning as well as education relating to dying and death. Staff should be familiar with the client's life story, past experiences, cultural or religious beliefs and family tradi-tions, as well as who their social worker, doctor and significant other people are.

Guidance for good practice
Education for people with autism

People with autism need to receive information regarding the definition of death. Specific terms should be used, for example 'fatally ill' rather than 'poorly' or 'sick'. Similarly, specific forms of address should be used, e.g. if the dead person was known to the person with autism as 'Nan', then that term of reference should be used at all times. In describing accidental death, sentences such as 'Their body was so badly hurt, the doctor couldn't make it better' and the 'body stopped working' can be helpful (Allison 2007). Euphemisms should *not* be used such as 'He has just gone to sleep'.

Explanations need to be simple and factual using everyday examples. People with autism often need to understand the facts about death. Some crematoriums have open days where you can go and see exactly what happens when the body is moved beyond the curtain. Similarly, seeing the coffin go down into the earth can help people on the spectrum understand that the person who has died is not coming back.

As part of educating people with autism on this topic it can be useful to develop some rules about how to behave at a funeral. Guidelines on what happens during the service or showing a video of a funeral can help. Checking on a person's desire for knowledge and using open-ended questions, e.g. 'How do you feel?' rather than 'Do you feel OK?' will enable the carer continuously to gauge the extent to which the person with autism can take talking about the death. Staff should not try to 'jolly individuals up' or try to 'make them laugh' but should empathize with them. The use of different faces may be used to ascertain the fluctuating feelings of someone with a verbal communication difficulty (see Worksheet 5.2).

The wide variation in the capabilities of people with autism introduces an additional complexity into the functions of staff offering support to bereaved clients. For example, an able person on the continuum might require detailed explanations and opportunities to explore their own concepts of death and after-life beliefs. The majority of people with ASC and those in the middle of the range will probably derive most comfort from simple, factual, directive language. Those at the lower end may need simplified information accompanied by pictures and symbols.

It can be helpful to set up a Bereavement Support Group which includes staff, family, local clergy, members of CRUSE, the Society of Compassionate Friends, The Samaritans, the British Humanist Association or National Secular Society (in the USA, the equivalent would include: the Association for Death Education and Counseling; Counseling for Loss and Life Changes; Crisis Grief and Healing, Maryland; Grief and Loss Resource Center; and in Australia – Seasons for Growth and Centre for Grief Education). Such a group can help train staff in areas such as: preparation of individuals for future loss, knowledge about how to manage bereavement and undertake practical arrangements, and helping individuals and their families receive the support they need. Such training may pre-empt problems associated with bereavement. Useful training resources include *Understanding Grief* (Hollins and Sireling 1999), *When Dad Died* (Hollins and Sireling 1989), Somerset Total Communication *Bereavement Pack* (Knight 2006), and publications from CRUSE and Jessica Kingsley Publishers.

Participating in rituals

There is a need for the person with autism to be involved in the ceremony or rituals of death, even if it is just to lay a wreath on the coffin. It is also often important for the person with autism to 'see the dead body' to help them understand that death is irreversible and the person is not coming back. Visiting the venue beforehand can give the person time to become familiar with it and allows an opportunity to identify any sensory issues they may have on the day. Strategies for leaving the venue should the person need to escape can be discussed and agreed upon.

Supporting individuals to develop coping strategies

The role of staff is to be there when needed, anticipate reactions, listen and read cues, intervene, ask how the person feels, talk about the deceased, and explain the grieving process. Developing memory books including photographs, pictures or objects of reference, such as a memento of the deceased person, are useful in enabling positive memories to be discussed. Writing letters, drawing pictures or playing songs that the loved one enjoyed can also help some people. Supporting the person to keep a 'feelings diary' (see Worksheet 5.2) to aid dealing with feelings may also be beneficial. Similarly, commemorating events such as anniversary days by developing a ritual (e.g. putting flowers on the grave, visiting the place where the ashes were scattered, making a memorial by planting a tree or flower bed, or sending the person a card) can help to provide the person with autism with an appropriate time to remember the deceased. This can also help to manage obsessive behaviours.

The use of external support can also be extremely useful. People with autism associate particular roles with specific people (e.g. vicar with funeral), so one way of stopping obsessional preoccupation with death is to confine talking about the subject to the appropriate person (see Raji and Hollins 2003). Where appropriate, form a circle of support, open to all people who have been bereaved, where an understanding of loss and emotional responses can be taught and ways of coping developed, or encourage them to join local support groups. Otherwise, helping them to find friends who will be supportive will help.

Case study – Guy

Guy has autism and recently lost his mother. He now lives with his retired dad and sister. Soon after his mum's funeral, he began to break up the furniture in his room. Starting with scratching the legs of a chair with a pen, Guy then began to lift his bedside table up with everything on it and drop it. This would happen every night for about two hours. Eventually the bedside table smashed and Guy turned to the headboard of his bed, carving lines in the wood. Guy's behaviour was extremely challenging to his father, who was still grieving the loss of his wife. Guy's father considered putting Guy in a residential home because he felt he could not cope. After about a month of this behaviour, Guy's key worker Jake asked Guy if he wanted to attend a local boxing club. This was a risk, as Guy had never really shown any interest in this sport before. However, it was decided that, since Guy got on well with his key worker and even if Guy didn't box, the 'trip out' to the boxing club would be beneficial in getting him out of the house (as well as providing respite for his dad). In the event, Guy did box a few times and enjoyed it very much, and whilst his challenging behaviour did not immediately stop, some of the frustration he was obviously feeling was filtered out.

Finally, where possible, continue routines, including helping the person to see friends whilst at the same time keeping decision-making to a minimum, allowing them to relinquish responsibilities if they need to. Returning to an activity, including going to work or a day centre after a bereavement, can be very stressful for people with autism. While a structured timetable can offer both relief and security from the overwhelmingly painful situation at home for some, for others it increases their anxiety about the grieving parent left, perhaps alone at home.

Just as we described in Chapter 1, anger may be directed at the one who died for abandoning the bereaved. It may also be directed at the person who broke the news of the death or it may be generalized. Anger may also arise when activities provided by the deceased are no longer available. Staff should enable individuals to express this anger without harming themselves or others, or damaging property, for example by doing exercise or using a punch bag. The case study above illustrates this point.

Finally, as with all of the fact sheets and worksheets with exercises in this resource, not all of them will be suitable or help everyone on the autistic spectrum who is suffering from a loss. Some of the exercises below require a certain level of comprehension. Also, do not be surprised if the person does not react at all initially, or reacts in what you would interpret as an inappropriate way (Read 1998). Again, we use symbols from Somerset Total Communication to illustrate our exercises but advise that each exercise should be individualized, using appropriate resources which may or may not include the symbols provided below, photographs, illustrations, drawings, etc. We wish you well with helping people with autism successfully move through their loss.

Fact Sheet 6.1

Loss through death

It is natural to feel sad and upset when someone you love dies.

There has been very little written about death and bereavement and autism.

Each individual has different reactions, but if you have autism you may go through similar stages of grief that people without autism go through when someone they love dies (see Fact Sheet 1.1 for these).

When someone dies you may:

think that it was your fault – guilt (but it was not your fault),

feel unwell, be unable to eat,

be awake at night, get headaches,

and need to go to the toilet more than usual.

Or you may not feel anything for a while – this is called

delayed shock.

When someone who used to help (e.g. a care manager) dies

you will wonder 'Who will help me now?'

So, when someone you love dies you need:

lots of social support/help,

someone to explain what death means,

and a place and time to remember the person.

You need to be able to go to the funeral

and participate in the funeral if you want to

(e.g. laying a wreath on the coffin).

You need to have people (a group) to talk to.

If you do not feel any better after a few months, you may need to see a

doctor to check if you are OK.

The doctor may give you some medicine to help you with your

depression.

A few **Do's** and **Don'ts** for staff/carers:

Do:

- offer time (brief but regular meetings can mean a lot – for some people, the perception of having support is as good as actual support)
- be available to listen
- talk about good and bad memories
- accept a person's feelings
- say 'I don't know' in relation to questions you really don't know the answer to such as 'Where have they [dead person] gone?'
- allow people to cry
- watch for behaviour changes
- be aware of previous bereavements and/or depression
- be sensitive to beliefs and cultural backgrounds
- work through the exercises below.

Don't:

- assume that the person with autism can cope without support
- think they do not 'feel' the loss
- deny their thoughts or views on the death
- use clichés such as 'You need to be strong' or 'You are coping well'
- make new or sudden changes to their regime
- think that you cannot support them.

Worksheet 6.1

Why people die

Aim: to discuss what death is and why it happens. Ultimately we are trying to help the person with autism:

- accept the loss
- express his or her feelings
- accept his or her feelings as normal
- live independently without the loved one.

Objective: to understand that death is final. The person or thing is not coming back. Once someone is dead they will always be dead.

Exercise: Why people die

Use the following sentences for discussion

People **die** when they are fatally ill and the doctor cannot make them better.

People who die might be old and their bodies no longer work.

People who die might have had an accident (e.g. a fall) and their bodies are broken. Their bodies cannot be mended.

Fatal means they will not get better. They will die.

When someone is alive they can breathe.

When someone or something is dead they cannot breathe

(e.g. dead bird)

(e.g. dead dog).

If someone cannot breathe and they are dead, they cannot do these things:

They cannot look around.

They cannot see you.

Their heart does not work.

They cannot hear you and you cannot hear them.

They cannot talk to you and you cannot talk to them.

They cannot feel hot or cold.

They cannot touch cold things.

They cannot touch hot things.

They cannot feel sick.

They cannot feel pain.

Now let's recall our conversation (tick the right boxes):

When someone is dead they see you.	**True** ☐	**False** ☐
When someone is dead you see them.	**True** ☐	**False** ☐
When someone is dead they hear you.	**True** ☐	**False** ☐
When someone is dead you hear them.	**True** ☐	**False** ☐
When someone is dead they talk to you.	**True** ☐	**False** ☐
When someone is dead you talk to them.	**True** ☐	**False** ☐
When someone is dead they feel hot or cold.	**True** ☐	**False** ☐
When someone is dead they feel hurt or sick.	**True** ☐	**False** ☐

Worksheet 6.2

What happens after a person dies

Aim: to teach the person step by step the process of burial, cremation, etc.

Objective: to help the person with autism understand what happens after a person dies.

Below is an example of how to do this exercise. It is a Christian example, but can be easily modified to make it relevant to different faiths.

Exercise: What happens after a person dies

After a person dies there is a funeral. Friends and family go to the funeral to remember the dead person.

At the funeral a person in a coffin is either cremated

or buried in a grave.

People sometimes put a wreath on the grave.

Activity on cremation

When a person is cremated their body is put in a coffin and burnt. Their ashes are then put in a small hole in the ground.

Task: Visit a crematorium – get a guided tour and fill in the following.

1. Look at the grave where the ashes are put. Look at the flowers on the grave – what colour are the flowers?

2. What happens at the cremation?

Activity on burial

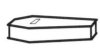 

When a person is buried their body is put in a coffin.

It is then put in a large hole in the ground in a graveyard.

Task: Visit a graveyard – look at the graves and fill in the following.

1.   What is in the graves?

2.   Why do people put flowers on the graves?

Worksheet 6.3

Discussing behaviour at a funeral

(This exercise can be adapted to suit the particular culture/religion of the person.)

Aim: to watch a video of a funeral. This can be a funeral that has taken place on the person's favourite soap opera (e.g. *EastEnders* or *Neighbours* or *Desperate Housewives*) or a purely educational video.

Objective: to discuss and prepare how a person should behave at a funeral according to social norms of the society/community.

Exercise: Discussing behaviour at a funeral

1.   What happens at a funeral?

2.   How do people behave?

Don't hit.

Don't pinch.

Don't swear.

Be nice.

3.   How should I behave?

4.   What should I do if I get upset?

Worksheet 6.4
Sharing feelings

Aim: to discuss feelings people have when someone has died.

Objective: to help the person with autism understand that their feelings are natural and to help them identify and express these feelings appropriately at different stages of the grieving process (use in conjunction with Figure 1.2 in Chapter 1).

Exercise: Sharing feelings

Let's talk about our feelings. When someone dies we might feel certain things. Tell me if you felt any of the following feelings or if you did any of the following things (insert pictures to match words).

Stage 1: Denial

Denial. We cannot believe that they have died.

We feel confused.

We feel lost.

These feelings might make us do things:

We forget they have gone. Where are they?

We look for them. Where are they? Where have they gone?

We can't concentrate.

We might behave in a way we don't usually.

185

Stage 2: Anger
We might feel:

angry – we are angry at them for leaving us,

guilty – we think it is our fault that they have died,

fear,

worry, be upset or distressed,

anxious, nervous, panicky, frustrated.

These feelings might make us:

have a headache/pain, be upset or ditressed.

We might be cross and argue with people.

We might cry.

We might smash things up, or rip our clothes, rip other people's clothes, swipe our food,

wet our pants,

be rude to people,

hate people,

stamp and spit,

be jealous of other people.

Stage 3: Despair
We might feel:

sad,

shy,

anxious, depressed,

fed up,

lonely.

These feeling, might make us:

tired, unable to sleep,

unable to talk to people,

unable to eat,

cry,

have nightmares – get a fright.

We can't do things as well as we usually can.

Stage 4: Adjustment
When we get support we might still feel:

confused,

more relaxed,

comfortable.

These feelings mean we can do things we used to do and new things:

make the bed,

go shopping,

go horse riding,

get excited,

feel like doing fun things,

be happy.

Worksheet 6.5

Moving on: Practical strategies for helping individuals live with grief

Aim: to find appropriate activities to move on to the final stage of grief, e.g. adjustment.

Objective: to enable the person to adjust and live with their loss.

If repetitive talking about the person they have lost becomes problematic, provide the individual with autism with a specific and regular time, place and person with whom they can discuss the issues. This can help to manage the repetitive/obsessive behaviour.

Exercise: Moving on: Practical strategies for helping individuals live with grief

1. Support the person to construct a feelings diary (similar to the exercise contained in Worksheet 5.2).

2. Enable the person to develop a memory book or box. This might include photographs, pictures or objects of reference such as a memento of the deceased person. The memory books/boxes can then be used to enable positive memories to be discussed.

3. Develop a way of remembering anniversary days by developing a ritual such as putting flowers on the grave, visiting the place where the ashes were scattered or making a memorial by planting a tree or flower bed.

4. If the deceased person supported the individual in a particular way, then help them to identify who is going to do those things for them now (see the exercises contained in Worksheets 4.2, 4.3 and 4.4).

5. If repetitive talking about the person they have lost becomes problematic, provide the individual with autism with a specific and regular time, place and person with whom they can discuss the issues. This can help to manage the repetitive/obsessive behaviour.

Thank you for reading our book.

Goodbye

References

Alexander, N.C. and Wiley, M.G. (1981) 'Situated activity and identity formation.' In M. Rosenberg and R. Turner (eds) *Sociological Perspectives on Social Psychology*. New York: Basic Books.

Allison, H.G. (1992) *The Management of Bereavement in Services for People with Autism*. London: National Autistic Society.

Allison, H.G. (2001) *Support for the Bereaved and Dying in Services for Adults with Autistic Spectrum Disorders*. London: National Autistic Society.

Allison, H.G. (2007) *The Management of Bereavement in Services for People with Autism*. London: National Autistic Society.

American Association on Intellectual and Developmental Disabilities (2007) *Fact Sheet: Person Centered Planning*, www.aamr.org/Policies/faq_planning.shtml

Angermeyer, M.C., Schulze, B. and Dietrich, S. (2003) 'Courtesy stigma – a focus group study of relatives of schizophrenia patients.' *Social Psychiatry and Psychiatric Epidemiology 38*, 593–602.

Arscott, K., Dagnan, D. and Kroese, B. (1998) 'Consent to psychological research by people with an intellectual disability.' *Journal of Applied Research in Intellectual Disabilities 11*, 1, 77–83.

Ashman, B. and Beadle-Brown, J. (2006) *A Valued Life: Developing Person-centred Approaches So People Can Be More Included*. London: United Response.

Asperger, H. (1944) 'Die "autistischen Psychopathen" im Kindesalter.' *Nervenkrankheiten 117*, 76–136 (English translation in Frith 1991).

Attwood, T. (1998) *Asperger's Syndrome: A Guide for Parents and Professionals*. London: Jessica Kingsley Publishers.

Attwood, T. (2006) *The Complete Guide to Asperger's Syndrome*. London: Jessica Kingsley Publishers.

Bank-Mikkelson, N. (1980) 'Denmark.' In R. Flynn and K. Nitsch (eds) *Normalisation, Social Integration and Community Services*. Baltimore, MD: University Park Press.

Barnett, M.M. (2002) 'Effect of breaking bad news on patients' perceptions of doctors.' *Journal of the Royal Society of Medicine 95*, 7, 343–347.

Bauminger, N. and Kasari, C. (2000) 'Loneliness and friendship in high-functioning children with autism.' *Journal of Child Development 7*, 2, 447–456.

Bauminger, N. and Shulman, C. (2003) 'The development and maintenance of friendship in high-functioning children with autism – Maternal perceptions.' *Autism 7*, 1, 81–97.

Bicknell, J. (1983) 'The psychopathology of handicap.' *British Journal of Medical Psychology 56*, 167–178.

Bigby, C. (2004) *Ageing with a Lifelong Disability: A Guide to Practice, Program and Policy Issues for Human Services Professionals*. London: Jessica Kingsley Publishers.

Bigelow, B.J. and LaGaipa, J.J. (1975) 'Children's written descriptions of friendship: A multidimensional analysis.' *Developmental Psychology 11*, 1, 105–116.

Blackman, N. (ed.) (1999) *Living with Loss: Helping People with Learning Disabilities Cope with Bereavement and Loss*. Brighton: Pavilion.

Blackman, N. (2003) *Loss and Learning Disability*. London: Worth.

Bloom, J. (2005) 'Breaking bad news.' In G. Grant, P. Goward, M. Richardson and P. Ramcharan (eds) *Learning Disability: A Life Cycle Approach to Valuing People.* Maidenhead: Open University Press.

Botsford, A. (2000) 'Integrating end of life care into services for people with an intellectual disability.' *Social Work in Health Care 31*, 35–48.

Botsford, A. (2004) 'The status of end of life care in organizations providing services for older people with a developmental disability.' *American Journal of Mental Retardation 109*, 349–443.

Botsford, A. and King, A. (2005) 'End of life care policies for people with intellectual disabilities.' *Journal of Disability Policy Studies 16*, 1, 22–30.

Bowlby, J. (1944) 'Forty-four juvenile thieves: The characters and home life.' *International Journal of Psycho-Analysis 25*, 19–52, 107–127.

Bowlby, J. (1951) *Maternal Care and Mental Health.* Geneva: World Health Organization.

Brelstaff, K. (1984) 'Reactions to death: Can the mentally handicapped grieve? Some experiences of those who did.' *Teach Train 22*, 10–16.

Brown, H., Burns, S. and Flynn, M. (2002) 'Supporting people through terminal illness and death.' In Foundation for People with Learning Disabilities: *Today and Tomorrow.* London: Mental Health Foundation.

Buckman, R. (1992) *How to Break Bad News: A Guide for Health Professionals.* London: Macmillan.

Burt, R.S. (1997) 'The contingent value of social capital.' *Administrative Science Quarterly 42*, 339–365.

Caldwell, P. (2002) *Learning the Language: A Video-based Resource on Building Relationships with People with Severe Learning Disabilities.* Brighton: Pavilion.

Caltabiano, M. and Sarafino, E. (2002) *Health Psychology: Biopsychosocial Interactions.* Chichester: Wiley.

Cambridge, P. (1999) 'The first hit: A case study of the physical abuse of people with learning disabilities and challenging behaviours in a residential service.' *Disability and Society 14*, 3, 285–308.

Cambridge, P., Carpenter, J., Beecham, J., Hallam, A., Knapp, M., Forrester-Jones, R. and Tate, A. (2001) *Twelve Years On: The Outcomes and Costs of Community Care for People with Learning Disabilities and Mental Health Problems.* Report for the Department of Health Outcomes of Social Care for Adults Initiative.

Cambridge, P., Carpenter, J., Beecham, J., Hallam, A., Knapp, M., Forrester-Jones, R. and Tate, A. (2002) 'Twelve years on: The long-term outcomes and costs of deinstitutionalisation and community care for people with learning disabilities.' *Tizard Learning Disability Review 7*, 34–42.

Cambridge, P. and Forrester-Jones, R. (2003) 'Using individualised communication for interviewing people with intellectual disability: A case study of user-centred research.' *Journal of Intellectual and Developmental Disability 28*, 1, 5–23.

Cambridge, P., Hayes, L., Knapp, M., Gould, E. and Fenyo, A. (1994) *Care in the Community: Five Years On.* Aldershot: Ashgate.

Cassel, J. (1976) 'The contribution of the social environment to host resistance.' *American Journal of Epidemiology 104*, 2, 107–123.

Cathcart, R. (1994a) *Understanding Death and Dying – Your Feelings.* Kidderminster: British Institute of Learning Disabilities.

Cathcart, R. (1994b) *Understanding Death and Dying – A Guide for Carers and Other Professionals.* Kidderminster: British Institute of Learning Disabilities.

Cathcart, R. (1994c) *Understanding Death and Dying – A Guide for Families and Friends.* Kidderminster: British Institute of Learning Disabilities.

Cesaroni, L. and Garber, M. (1991) 'Exploring the experience of autism through firsthand accounts.' *Journal of Autism and Developmental Disorders 21*, 303–314.

Chadsey, J. and Beyer, S. (2001) 'Social relationships in work settings.' *Mental Retardation and Developmental Disabilities Research Reviews 1*, 122–127.

Chamberlain, B., Kasari, C. and Rotheram-Fuller, E. (2007) 'Involvement or isolation? The social networks of children with autism in regular classrooms.' *Journal of Autism and Developmental Disorders 37*, 2, 230–242.

Chisholm, M. (2002) *Such Silver Currents: The Story of William and Lucy Clifford 1845–1929.* Cambridge: The Lutterworth Press.

Clements, J. (2005) *People with Autism Behaving Badly.* London: Jessica Kingsley Publishers.

REFERENCES

Clements, J. and Zarkowska, E. (2000) *Behavioural Concerns and Autistic Spectrum Disorders: Explanations and Strategies for Change.* London: Jessica Kingsley Publishers.

Conboy-Hill, S. (1992) 'Grief, loss and people with learning disabilities.' In S. Conboy-Hill and A. Waitman (eds) *Psychotherapy and Mental Handicap.* London: Sage.

Cooke, L. (1997) 'Cancer and learning disability.' *Journal of Intellectual Disability Research 41,* 4, 312–316.

Craft, M. and Craft, A. (1979) *Handicapped Married Couples.* London: Routledge & Kagan Paul.

Cummins, R.A. and Lau, A.L.D. (2003) 'Community integration or community exposure? A review and discussion in relation to people with an intellectual disability.' *Journal of Applied Research in Intellectual Disabilities 16,* 2, 145–157.

Currer, C. (2001) *Responding to Grief: Dying, Bereavement and Social Care.* Basingstoke: Palgrave.

Department of Health (2001a) *Seeking Consent: Working with People with Learning Disabilities.* London: Department of Health.

Department of Health (2001b) *Valuing People: A New Strategy for Learning Disability for the 21st Century.* London: Department of Health.

Dilk, M.N. and Bond, G.R. (1996) 'Meta-analytic evaluation of skills training research for individuals with severe mental illness.' *Journal of Consulting and Clinical Psychology 64,* 1337–1346.

Dodd, K. and Gathard, J. (1998) *Feeling Poorly.* Brighton: Pavilion.

Donenberg, G. and Baker, B. (1993) 'The impact of young children with externalizing behaviors on their families.' *Journal of Abnormal Child Psychology 21,* 179–198.

Downer, J. (2000) 'Sharing my history and experience.' *Journal of Intellectual Disability Research 44,* 308.

Eurelings-Bontekoe, E., Diestra, R. and Verschuur, M. (1995) 'Psychological distress, social support, and social support seeking: A prospective study among primary mental health care patients.' *Society, Science and Medicine 40,* 1083–1089.

Evenhuis, H. (2001) *People with Intellectual Disability: Normal Citizens, Exceptional Patients. Initiative to Research Policy.* Rotterdam: Erasmus University Rotterdam.

Felce, D. and Perry, J. (1995) 'Quality of life: Its definition and measurement.' *Research in Developmental Disabilities 16,* 1, 51–74.

Forrester-Jones, R. (1998) *Social Networks and Social Support: Development of an Instrument.* Departmental Working Paper, Tizard Centre, Canterbury, University of Kent.

Forrester-Jones, R. (2001) 'Friendships and social integration through leisure.' Commentary. *Tizard Learning Disability Review 6,* 4, 28–32.

Forrester-Jones, R. (2004) 'What do people with learning disabilities think about funerals?' *Journal of Intellectual Disability Research 48,* 436.

Forrester-Jones, R. and Barnes, A. (in press) 'On being a girlfriend not a patient: The quest for an acceptable identity amongst people diagnosed with a severe mental illness.' *Journal of Mental Health.*

Forrester-Jones, R., Cambridge, P., Carpenter, J., Tate, A., Beecham, J., Hallam, A., Knapp, M., Coolen-Schrijner, P. and Wooff, D. (2006) 'The social networks of people with learning disabilities living in the community twelve years after resettling from long-stay hospital.' *Journal of Applied Research in Intellectual Disability 19,* 285–295.

Forrester-Jones, R., Carpenter, J., Cambridge, P., Tate, P., Hallam, A., Knapp, M. and Beecham, J. (2002) 'The quality of life of people twelve years after resettlement from long-stay hospitals: Users' views on their living environment, daily activities and future aspirations.' *Disability and Society 17,* 7, 741–758.

Forrester-Jones, R. and Duplock, L. (in progress) The Social Network Guide: An Instrument to Measure and Understand the Social Networks of People with Mental Health Difficulties, People with Learning Disabilities and People with Autism.

Forrester-Jones, R. and Grant, G. (1997) *Resettlement from Large Psychiatric Hospital to Small Community Residence.* Aldershot: Avebury.

Forrester-Jones, R., Jones, S., Heason, S. and Di'Terlizzi, M. (2004) 'Supported employment: A route to social networks.' *Journal of Applied Research in Intellectual Disabilities 17,* 1–10.

Foucault, M. (1990) *The History of Sexuality. Vol. 1: An Introduction.* Translated by Robert Hurley. New York: Pantheon Books.

Freud, S. (1961) 'Mourning and melancholia.' In J. Strachey (ed. and trans) *The Standard Edition of the Complete Psychological Works of Sigmund Freud* (14) London: Hogarth Press.

Frender, S. and Schiffmiller, R. (2007) *Me, My Emotions, and My Brother with Asperger's Syndrome.* London: Jessica Kingsley Publishers.

Frith, U. (1989) *Autism: Explaining the Enigma.* Oxford: Blackwell.

Frith, U. (1991) *Autism and Asperger Syndrome.* Cambridge: Cambridge University Press.

Gammeltoft, L. and Nordenhof, M.S. (2007) *Autism, Play and Social Interaction.* London: Jessica Kingsley Publishers.

Gates, B. (ed.) (1986) *Learning Disabilities: Towards Inclusion.* London: Churchill Livingstone.

Gillberg, C. and Billstedt, E. (2000) 'Autism and Asperger syndrome: Coexistence with other clinical disorders.' *Acta Psychiatria Scandinavica 102*, 321–330.

Goffman, E. (1959) *The Presentation of Self in Everyday Life.* New York: Doubleday Anchor.

Goffman, E. (1962a) *Asylums.* New York: Anchor.

Goffman, E. (1962b) *Stigma.* Englewood Cliffs, NJ: Prentice-Hall.

Gordon, S. (1972) 'Missing in special education: Sex Symposium No. 6.' *Journal of Special Education 5*, 351–381.

Grandin, T. (1995) *Thinking in Pictures.* New York: Doubleday.

Grannoveter, M.S. (1995) *Getting a Job: A Study of Contacts and Careers* (2nd edition). Chicago: University of Chicago Press.

Grant, G. (2005) 'Healthy and successful ageing.' In G. Grant, P. Goward, M. Richardson and P. Ramcharan (eds) *Learning Disability: A Life Cycle Approach to Valuing People.* Maidenhead: Open University Press.

Grant, G., Goward, P., Richardson, M. and Ramcharan, P. (eds) (2005) *Learning Disability: A Life Cycle Approach to Valuing People.* Maidenhead: Open University Press.

Grant, G. and Ramcharan, P. (2005) 'Making a life in the community. Is intensive personalized support enough?' In G. Grant, P. Goward, M. Richardson and P. Ramcharan (eds) *Learning Disability: A Life Cycle Approach to Valuing People.* Maidenhead: Open University Press.

Gutstein, S.E. and Sheely, R.K. (2002) *Relationship Development Intervention with Children, Adolescents and Adults.* London: Jessica Kingsley Publishers.

Harper, D.C. and Wadsworth, J.S. (1993) 'Grief in adults with mental retardation: Preliminary finding.' *Research in Developmental Disabilities 14*, 4, 313–330.

Hatzidimitriadou, E. and Forrester-Jones, R. (2002) *The Needs of Older People with Learning Disabilities and Mental Health Difficulties in the Medway Area.* Canterbury: Tizard Centre.

Heller, T. (2002) 'Residential settings and outcomes for individuals with intellectual disabilities.' *Current Opinion in Psychiatry 15*, 5, 503–508.

Hewett, D. and Nind, M. (eds) (1998) *Interaction in Action: Reflections on the Use of Intensive Interaction.* London: David Fulton Publishers.

Hobson, R. and Lee, A. (1998) 'Hello and goodbye: A study of social gaze in autism.' *Journal of Autism and Developmental Disorders 28*, 117–127.

Hollins, S. (1993) 'Group analytic therapy for people with a mental handicap.' In S. Conboy-Hill and A. Waitman (eds) *Psychotherapy and Mental Handicap.* London: Sage.

Hollins. S. and Sireling, L. (1989) *When Dad Died.* London: St George's Hospital.

Hollins. S. and Sireling, L. (1999) *Understanding Grief, Working with Grief and People Who Have Learning Disabilities* (2nd edition). Brighton: Pavilion; and London: St George's Hospital.

Hollins, S. and Tuffrey-Wijne, I. (2005) 'Promoting healthy lifestyles.' In G. Grant, P. Goward, M. Richardson and P. Ramcharan (eds) *Learning Disability: A Life Cycle Approach to Valuing People.* Maidenhead: Open University Press.

Howard, B., Cohn, E. and Orsmond, G. (2006) 'Understanding and negotiating friendships: Perspectives from an adolescent with Asperger syndrome.' *Autism 10*, 6, 619–627.

Hurlbutt, K. and Chalmers, L. (2002) 'Adults with autism speak out: Perceptions of their life experiences.' *Focus on Autism and Other Developmental Disorders 17*, 2, 103–111.

Jancar, J.W. (1990) 'Cancer and mental handicap.' *British Journal of Psychiatry 156*, 531–533.

REFERENCES

Jenner, P. and Gale, T.M. (2006) 'A relationship support service for people with learning disabilities.' *Tizard Learning Disability Review 11*, 2, 18–25.

Johnson, H.M. (2003) 'Unspeakeable conversations: The case for my life.' *New York Times Magazine 16*, 152.

Jones, J. (2000) 'A total communication approach towards meeting the communication needs of people with learning disabilities.' *Tizard Learning Disability Review 5*, 1, 20–26.

Jones, R. and Meldal, T. (2001) 'Social relationships in Asperger's syndrome.' *Journal of Learning Disabilities 5*, 1, 35–41.

Kanner, L. (1943) 'Autistic disturbances of affective contact.' *Nervous Child 2*, 217–250.

Kempton, W. (1972) *Guidelines for Planning a Training Course on Human Sexuality and the Retarded.* Philadelphia, PA: Planned Parenthood Association of Southern Pennsylvania.

Kitching, N. (1987) 'Helping people with mental handicaps cope with bereavement.' *Mental Handicap 15*, 60–63.

Klass, D., Silverman, P.R. and Nickman, S.L. (1996) *Continuing Bonds: New Understandings of Grief.* Philadelphia: Taylor and Francis.

Knight, L. (2006) *Bereavement Pack.* Bridgewater: Somerset Total Communication in partnership with Resources for Learning.

Knott, R., Lewis, C. and Williams, T. (1995) 'Sibling interaction in children with learning disabilities: A comparison of autism and Down's syndrome.' *Journal of Child Psychology and Psychiatry 36*, 965–975.

Kübler-Ross, E. (1970) *On Death and Dying.* London: Tavistock Routledge.

Lawson, J. (2003) 'Depth accessibility difficulties: An alternative conceptualisation of autism spectrum conditions.' *Journal for the Theory of Social Behaviour 33*, 189–202.

Lawson, W. (2001) *Understanding and Working with the Spectrum of Autism: An Insider's View.* London: Jessica Kingsley Publishers.

Lawson, W. (2006) *Friendships: The Aspie Way.* London: Jessica Kingsley Publishers.

Leekam, S., Baron-Cohen, S., Perrett, D., Milders, M. and Brown, S. (1997) 'Eye-direction detection: A dissociation between geometric and joint attention skills in autism.' *Journal of Developmental Psychology 15*, 77–95.

Lemert, E. (1951) *Social Pathology.* New York: McGraw-Hill.

Leslie, A. (1987) 'Pretense and representation: The origins of "theory of mind".' *Psychological Review 94*, 412–426.

Leslie, A. and Roth, D. (1993) 'What autism teaches us about metarepresentation.' In S. Baron-Cohen, H. Tager-Flusberg and D.J. Cohen (eds) *Understanding Other Minds: Perspectives from Autism.* Oxford: Oxford University Press.

Llewellyn, G. and McConnell, D. (2002) 'Mothers with learning disabilities and their support networks.' *Journal of Intellectual Disability Research 46*, 1, 17–34.

Lewis, C.S. (1961) *A Grief Observed.* London: Faber and Faber.

Leyer, O., Folstein, S., Bacalman, S., Davis, N., Dinh, E., Morgan, J., Tager-Flusberg, H. and Lainhart, J. (2006) 'Comorbid psychiatric disorders in children with autism: Interview development and rates of disorders.' *Journal of Autism and Developmental Disorders 36*, 7, 849–861.

Lin, N. and Dean, A. (1985) 'Social support in the etiology of depression: A panel study.' *Psychiatry: The State of the Art 7*, 123–128.

Long, R. (2005) *Loss and Separation.* London: David Fulton Publishers.

Lyttle, A. (2001) Lecture on 'Bereavement and Loss' presented to BSc students in Community Care Practice, University of Kent.

Maguire, P. (1998) 'Breaking bad news.' *European Journal of Surgical Oncology 24*, 3, 188–199.

Mansell, J. and Beadle-Brown, J. (2004) 'Person-centred planning or person-centred action? Policy and practice in intellectual disability services.' *Journal of Applied Research in Intellectual Disabilities 17*, 1, 1–9.

Mansell, J., Beadle-Brown, J., Ashman, B. and Ockendon, J. (2005) *Person-centred Active Support: A Multi-media Training Resource for Staff to Enable Participation, Inclusion and Choice for People with Learning Disabilities.* Brighton: Pavilion.

Marrone, M. (1998) *Attachment and Interaction.* London: Jessica Kingsley Publishers.

Martinson, I., Deck, E. and Adams, D. (1992) 'Ritual and mourning customs.' In J. Littlewood (ed.) *Aspects of Grief: Bereavement in Adult Life.* London: Tavistock Routledge.

McCarthy, M. (1999) *Sexuality and Women with Learning Disabilities.* London: Jessica Kingsley Publishers.

McConkey, R. (2005) 'Promoting friendships and developing social networks.' In G. Grant, P. Goward, M. Richardson and P. Rancharan (eds) *Learning Disability: A Life Cycle Approach to Valuing People.* Maidenhead: Open University Press.

McEnhill, L. (2004) 'Disability.' In D. Oliviere and B. Monroe (eds) *Death, Dying and Social Differences.* Oxford: Oxford University Press.

McEnhill, L.S. (2006) 'The role of hospices.' In S. Read (ed.) *Palliative Care for People with Learning Disabilities.* London: Quay Books.

McKechnie, R.C. (2006) 'What does the literature tell us about death, dying and palliative care for people with intellectual disabilities?' *Progress in Palliative Care 14,* 6, 255–259.

Mead, M. (1934) *Mind, Self and Society.* Chicago: University of Chicago Press.

Melberg Schwier, K. and Hingsburger, D. (2000) *Sexuality: Your Sons and Daughters with Intellectual Disabilities.* Baltimore, MD: Paul H. Brookes.

Mishler, E. (1999) *Storylines.* Cambridge, MA: Harvard University Press.

Mitchell, C. (2005) *Glass Half Empty, Glass Half Full: How Asperger's Syndrome Has Changed My Life.* London: Paul Chapman.

Molloy, C., Morrow, A., Meinzen-Derr, J., Dawson, G., Bernier, R., Dunn, M., Hyman, S., McMahon, W., Goudie-Nice, J., Hepburn, S., Minshew, N., Rogers, S., Sigman, M., Spence, M., Tager-Flusberg, H., Volkmar, F. and Lord, C. (2006) 'Familial autoimmune thyroid disease as a risk factor for regression in children with autism spectrum disorder: A CPEA study.' *Journal of Autism and Developmental Disorders 36,* 3, 317–324.

Moore, C. (2003) *George and Sam: Autism in the Family.* Harmondsworth: Penguin.

Moore, C. (2003) 'Mind the gap.' *The Guardian,* 14 May. www.guardian.co.uk/parents/story/0,,955251,00.html

Morris, C.D., Niederbuhl, J.M. and Mahr, J.M. (1993) 'Determining the capability of individuals with mental retardation to give informed consent.' *American Journal on Mental Retardation 98,* 263–272.

Mruk, C. (1999) *Self Esteem: Research Theory and Practice.* London: Free Association Books.

National Autistic Society (2003a) *Autism: The Demand for Advocacy.* London: National Autistic Society.

National Autistic Society (2003b) *Autism: Rights in Reality.* London: National Autistic Society.

Newcomb, A. and Bagwell, C. (1996) 'The developmental significance of children's friendship relations.' In W. Bukowski, A. Newcomb and W. Hartup (eds) *The Company They Keep.* Cambridge: Cambridge University Press.

O'Brien, J. (1987) 'A guide to life style planning: Using the activities catalogue to integrate services and natural support systems.' In B. Wilson and G. Bellamy (eds) *The Activities Catalogue: An Alternative Curriculum for Youth and Adults with Severe Disabilities.* Baltimore, MD: Paul H. Brookes.

O'Callaghan, A. and Murphy, G. (2002) *Capacity to Consent to Sexual Relationships in Adults with Learning Disabilities.* Final Report written for the Nuffield Foundation. Lancaster University.

Oliver, D., Forrester-Jones, R. and Duplock, L. (2007) 'Palliative care and intellectual disability: exploring the knowledge of specialist palliative care providers in Kent.' Presented at 10th Congress of the European Association for Palliative Care, Budapest, Hungary, 7–9 June.

Oswain, M. (1985) 'Bereavement.' In M. Craft, J. Bicknell and S. Hollins (eds) *Mental Handicap: A Multidisciplinary Approach.* London: Bailliere Tindall.

Oswain, M. (1991) *Am I Allowed to Cry? A Study of Bereavement Amongst People Who Have Learning Difficulties.* London: Human Horizons.

Painter, K.K. (2006) *Social Skills Groups for Children and Adolescents with Asperger's Syndrome: A Step-by-Step Program.* London: Jessica Kingsley Publishers.

Parkes, C.M. (1970) 'The first year of bereavement: A longitudinal study of the reaction of london widows to the death of their husbands.' *Psychiatry 33,* 444.

Parkes, C.M. (1993) 'Bereavement as a psycho-social transition: Processes of adaptation to change.' In M. Stroebe, W. Stroebe and R. Hanson (eds) *Handbook of Bereavement.* Cambridge: Cambridge University Press.

REFERENCES

Parkes, C.M., Launganik, P. and Young, B. (eds) (1997) *Death and Bereavement Across Cultures.* London: Routledge.

Patja, K. (2001) *Life Expectancy and Mortality in Intellectual Disability.* Helsinki: Finnish Association on Mental Retardation.

Phillips, L.L. and Cuthill, J.D. (2002) 'Breaking bad news: A clinician's view of the literature.' *Annals of the Royal College of Physicians and Surgeons of Canada 35,* 5, 287–293.

Phillips, M.R., Pearson, V., Li, F.F., Xu, V. and Yang, L. (2002) 'Stigma and expressed emotion: A study of people with schizophrenia and their family members in China.' *British Journal of Psychiatry 181,* 488–493.

Prus, R. (1975) 'Labeling theory: A reconceptualisation and propositional statement on typing.' *Sociological Focus 8,* 79–96.

Ptacek, J.T. and Ellison, N.M. (2000) 'Health care providers' perspectives on breaking bad news to patients.' *Critical Care Nursing Quarterly 23,* 2, 1–9.

Raitasuo, S., Virtanen, H. and Raitasuo, J. (1998) 'Anorexia nervosa, major depression and obsessive-compulsive disorder in a Down's syndrome patient.' *International Journal of Eating Disorders 23,* 107–109.

Raji, O. and Hollins, S. (2003) 'How far are people with learning disabilities involved with funeral rights?' *British Journal of Learning Disabilities 31,* 42–45.

Ramcharan, P., Roberts, G, Grant, G. and Borland, J. (eds) (1997) *Empowerment in Everyday Life: Learning Disability.* London: Jessica Kingsley Publishers.

Ramirez, A.J., Cull, A., Graham, J., Gregory, W.M., Leaning, M.S., Richards, M.A., Snashall, D.C. and Timothy, A.R. (1995) 'Burnout and psychiatric disorders among cancer clinicians.' *British Journal of Cancer 71,* 6, 1132–1133.

Rawlings, D.C. (2000) 'Bereavement and adults with autism in a residential setting.' *Good Autism Practice 1,* 1, 21–28.

Read, S. (1998) 'Breaking bad news to people with a learning disability.' *British Journal of Nursing 7,* 2, 86–91.

Read, S. (2006) (ed.) 'Counselling and support.' In S. Read (ed.) *Palliative Care for People with Learning Disabilities.* London: Quay Books Division.

Roberts, W., Weaver, L., Brian, J., Bryson, S., Emelianova, S. and Griffiths, A.M. (2001) 'Repeated doses of porcine secretin in the treatment of autism: A randomized, placebo-controlled trial.' *Pediatrics 107,* 5, E71.

Robertson, J. (1953) 'Some responses of young children to the loss of maternal care.' *Nursing Times 49,* 382–386.

Robertson, J., Emerson, E., Gregory, N., Hatton, C., Kessissoglou, S., Hallam, A. and Lineham, C. (2001) 'Social networks of people with mental retardation in residential settings.' *Mental Retardation 39,* 201–214.

Roeyers, H. and Mycke, K. (1995) 'Siblings of a child with autism, with mental retardation, and with a normal development.' *Child: Care, Health, and Development 21,* 305–319.

Rook, K.S. (1992) 'Detrimental aspects of social relationships: Taking stock of an emerging literature.' In H.O.F. Veiel and U. Baumann (eds) *The Meaning and Measurement of Social Support.* New York: Hemisphere.

Rutter, D. (1984) *Looking and Seeing: The Role of Visual Communication in Social Interaction.* Chichester: Wiley.

Sarason, I.G., Levine, H.M., Basham, R.B. and Sarason, B.R. (1983) 'Assessing social support: The Social Support Questionnaire.' *Journal of Personality and Social Support 44,* 127–139.

Schalock, R.L. (2004) 'The concept of quality of life: What we know and do not know.' *Journal of Intellectual Disability Research 48,* 3, 205.

Schneider, C.B. (2006) *Acting Antics: A Theatrical Approach to Teaching Social Understanding to Kids and Teens with Asperger Syndrome.* London: Jessica Kingsley Publishers.

Schwabenland, C. (1999) 'Introduction.' In C. Schwabenland (ed.) *Relationships in the Lives of People with Learning Difficulties.* The Elfrida Lectures 1997/1998. The Elfrida Society.

Seedhouse, D. (1986) *Health: The Foundations for Achievement.* Chichester: Wiley.

Sheldon, F. (1998) 'ABC of palliative care: Bereavement.' *British Medical Journal 316,* 456–458.

Singer, P. (1994) *Rethinking Life and Death: The Collapse of Our Traditional Ethics.* New York: St. Martin's Griffin.

Srivastava, A.K. (2001) 'Developing friendships and social integration through leisure for people with moderate, severe and profound ID transferred from hospital to community care.' *Tizard Learning Disability Review 6,* 19–27.

Stoddart, K. (1999) 'Adolescents with Asperger syndrome: Three case studies of individual and family therapy.' *Autism 3*, 3, 255–271.

St. Quintin, P. and Disney, J. (2003) 'Transition: The experiences of young people and their families in England.' *Tizard Learning Disability Review 8*, 29–32.

Strathdee, R. (2005) *Social Exclusion and the Remaking of Social Networks.* Aldershot: Ashgate.

Stroebe, M. and Schut, H. (1998) 'Culture and grief.' *Bereavement Care 17*, 1, 7–11.

Stroebe, M. and Schut, H. (1999) 'The dual process model of coping with bereavement: Rationale and description.' *Death Studies 23*, 197–224.

Stroebe, M., Stroebe, W. and Hansson, R. (eds) (1993) *Handbook of Bereavement: Theory, Research and Intervention.* New York: Cambridge University Press.

Stryker, S. (1968) 'Identity salience and role performance.' *Journal of Marriage and the Family 4*, 558–564.

Sudnow, D. (1967) *Passing On: The Social Organisation of Death.* Englewood Cliffs, NJ: Prentice Hall.

Swinton, J. (2001) *A Space to Listen: Meeting the Spiritual Needs for People with Learning Disabilities.* London: Mental Health Foundation.

Swinton, J. (2004) *No Box to Tick. A Booklet for Carers and Support Workers on Meeting the Spiritual Needs of People with Learning Disabilities.* London: Mental Health Foundation.

Swinton, J. and Powrie, E. (2004) *Why Are We Here? Meeting the Spiritual Needs of People with Learning Disabilities.* London: Mental Health Foundation.

Szivos, S. and Griffiths, E. (1990) 'Group processes involved in coming to terms with a mentally retarded identity.' *Mental Retardation 28*, 333–341.

Tammet, D. (2006) *Born on a Blue Day: A Memoir of Asperger's and an Extraordinary Mind.* London: Hodder and Stoughton.

Tarrier, N., Vaughn, C., Lader, M. and Leff, J. (1979) 'Bodily reactions to people and events in schizophrenics.' *Archives of General Psychiatry 36*, 3, 311–315.

Taylor, R. (1980) *Cultural Ways* (3rd edition). Boston, MA: Allyn & Bacon.

Todd, S. (2002) 'Death does not become us.' *Journal of Gerontology and Social Work 38*, 225–239.

Todd, S. (2005) 'Surprised endings: The dying of people with learning disabilities in residential services.' *International Journal of Palliative Nursing 11*, 2, 80–82.

Todd, S. and Blackman, N. (2005) 'Reconnecting death and learning disability.' *European Journal of Palliative Care 12*, 32–34.

Tracy, E.M. (1990) 'Identifying social support resources: At risk families.' *Social Work 35*, 252–258.

Tracy, E.M. and Bell, N.A. (1994) 'Social Network Map: Some further refinements on administration.' *Social Work Research 18*, 1, 56–60.

Tracy, E.M. and Whittaker, J.K. (1990) 'The Social Network Map: Assessing social support in clinical practice.' *Families in Society 71*, 8, 461–470.

Travis, L.L. and Sigman, M. (1998) 'Social deficits and interpersonal relationships in autism.' *Mental Retardation and Developmental Disabilities Reviews 4*, 65–72.

Tsakanikos, E., Sturmey, P., Costello, H., Holt, G. and Bouras, N. (2007) 'Referral trends in mental health services for adults with intellectual disability and autism spectrum disorders.' *Autism 11*, 1, 9–17.

Tuffrey-Wijne, I. (2003) 'The palliative care needs of people with intellectual disabilities: A literature review.' *Palliative Medicine 17*, 55–62.

Tuffrey-Wijne, I., Hollins, S. and Curfs, L. (2005) 'Supporting patients who have intellectual disabilities: A survey investigating staff training needs.' *International Journal of Palliative Nursing 11*, 4, 182–188.

Tyne, A. (1989) 'Building friendships, creating ties.' *Community Living*, April, 11–12.

Veenhoven, R. (1998) 'The utility of happiness.' *Social Indicators Research 20*, 333–354.

Vermeulen, P. (2000) *I am Special: Introducing Children and Young People to Their Autistic Spectrum Disorder.* London: Jessica Kingsley Publishers.

Wadsworth, J. and Harper, D. (1991) 'Grief and bereavement in mental retardation: A need for new understanding.' *Death Studies 15*, 281–292.

REFERENCES

Wall, K. (1998) *Friendship Skills and Opportunities among People with ID.* Social Work Monographs. University of East Anglia.

Walker, A., Walker, C. and Ryan, T. (1996) 'Older people with learning difficulties leaving institutional care – a case of double jeopardy.' *Ageing and Society 16,* 125–150.

Walter, T. (1994) *The Revival of Death.* London: Routledge.

Walter, T. (1996) 'A new model of grief: Bereavement and biography.' *Mortality 1,* 7–27.

Walter, T. (1999) *On Bereavement.* Buckingham: Open University Press.

Ward, L. (2001) *Considered Choices? The New Genetics, Prenatal Testing and People with Learning Disabilities.* Kidderminster: British Institute of Learning Disabilities.

Wayslenki, D.A., Goering, P.N., Lemire, D., Lindsey, S. and Lancee, W. (1993) 'The Hostel Outreach Program: Assertive case management for homeless mentally ill persons.' *Hospital and Community Psychiatry 44,* 9, 848–853.

Webb-Mitchell, B. (1994) *Unexpected Guests at God's Banquet: Welcoming People with Disabilities into the Church.* New York: Crossroad.

Wenger. G.C. (1984) *The Supportive Network: Coping with Old Age.* London: Allen and Unwin.

Whitman, T.L. (2004) *The Development of Autism: A Self-regulatory Perspective.* London: Jessica Kingsley Publishers.

Williams, D. (2006) *The Jumbled Jigsaw: An Insider's Approach to the Treatment of Autistic Spectrum 'Fruit Salads'.* London: Jessica Kingsley Publishers.

Wikan, U. (1988) 'Bereavement and loss in two Muslim communities: Egypt and Bali compared.' *Social Science and Medicine 27,* 5, 451–460.

Wing, L. and Gould, J. (1979) 'Severe impairments of social interaction and associated abnormalities in children: Epidemiology and classification.' *Journal of Autism and Developmental Disorders 9,* 1, 11–29.

Wing, L., Leekam, S.R., Libby, S.J., Gould, J. and Larcombe, M. (2002) 'The Diagnostic Interview for Social and Communication Disorders: Background, inter-rater reliability and clinical use.' *Journal of Child Psychology and Psychiatry 3,* 3, 307–325.

Wolfensberger, W. (1983) 'Social role valorization: a proposed new term for the principle of normalization.' *Mental Retardation 21,* 234–239.

Wolfensberger, W. and Glen, S. (1975) *PASS 3: Program Analysis of Service Systems: A Method for the Quantitative Evaluation of Human Services. A Handbook.* Toronto: NIMR.

World Health Organization (1987) *Mental Disorders: A Glossary and Guide to their Classification in Accordance with the 10th Revision of the International Classification of Diseases* (ICD-10). Geneva: World Health Organization.

Worden, W.J. (1991) *Grief Counselling and Grief Therapy: A Handbook for the Mental Health Practitioner* (2nd edition). New York: Springer.

Wortman, C.B. and Silver, R.C. (1989) 'The myths of coping with loss.' *Journal of Consulting and Clinical Psychology 57,* 349–357.

Yanok, J. and Beifus, J. (1993) 'Communicating about loss and mourning: Death education for individuals with mental retardation.' *Mental Retardation 31,* 144–147.

Useful websites

Autistic spectrum conditions

Autism Society of America: www.autism-society.org

Autism Research Institute: www.autism.org

National Autistic Society: www.nas.org.uk

Donna Williams' Website: www.donnawilliams.net

The Autism Source – A Global Information and Support Network: www.asperger.org

Tony Attwood's Website: www.tonyattwood.com.au

Person-centred planning

Helen Sanderson Associates: www.helensandersonassociates.co.uk

Paradigm: www.paradigm-uk.org

Learning disabilities

The American Association on Intellectual and Developmental Disabilities (AAIDD):
www.aamr.org

British Institute of Learning Disabilities: www.bild.org.uk

Bereavement

Cruse Bereavement Care: www.crusebereavementcare.org.uk

Bereavement Care Centre: www.bereavementcare.com.au

Bereavement in the Lives of People with Intellectual Disabilities:
www.intellectualdisability.info/lifestages/bereavement.htm

Positive behaviour support

Positive Behavioural Support Pack:
www.kent.ac.uk/tizard/SubscriberNet/positivebehaviouralsupport.doc